THE GOLDEN AVENUE:
THE HISTORY AND PEOPLE OF OCEAN AVENUE, AMITYVILLE, NY

DOUG ROBINSON

Printed in the United States of America

First Printing: October 2018

Lulu.com

978-0-359-09730-2

In memory of Bob and Grace Robinson,

my parents,who put us on Ocean Avenue in 1953

and planted the seed for this book.

Acknowledgements

Like all writers of history I owe much to those who came before me. I am especially indebted to Bill Lauder, Historian Emeritus of the Amityville Historical Society, for his book *Amityville History Revisited* (The Amityville Historical Society, 1992). His work provided much of the "bones" of Amityville history and let me focus on the stories centered around Ocean Avenue people.

Not all of the Ocean Avenue folks I wanted to write about were famous enough to have biographies written about them so I had to rely on childhood friends, some still closely tied to Amityville, to help me flesh out my stories. Some, like Kurt Nezbeda, Karen Nezbeda Yatuzis, Steve Brice and Bruce Parker, were not just contributors but became part of the narrative. Their input, through interviews, photos and running e-mail streams, was invaluable. I met Charlie (Bucky) Parker (no relation to Bruce) through an internet chat room about wooden boat building and marveled at how we lived so close together as kids but never knew each other. Bucky provided wonderful photos and stories about his Ocean Avenue family and friends which have greatly enhanced this book.

I was truly blessed to visit with Owen Brooks and his wife Marilyn in the early stages of my research. His sailing yarns helped the stories about the Ocean Avenue boat builders come alive. Sadly, he passed away a few months after we spoke.

Some of the photos come from Amityville folks I met or reconnected with through my research: Barth Keller, Thom Flemming, Don Thomson and Rudy Sittler. I am further indebted to Rudy for great insight into the early boat building days and for allowing me to use an image of one of his father's wonderful watercolors on the cover of the book. I have thoroughly enjoyed participating in the private Facebook page for Amityvillans hosted by Tommy Maher. It has been a great way to share memories of the town's bygone times. There is a continuing passion about Amityville's impact on our journeys to adulthood and the encouragement from the members of this group has been overwhelming.

I was very fortunate to get help and guidance from some great organizations. I spent time with Seth Purdy, curator for the Lauder Museum of the Amityville Historical Society. His knowledge of Amityville history was freely shared. The Long Island Maritime Museum in West Sayville, NY, has a great display of Great South Bay boats and a very comprehensive library on the subject. A number of the photos from the boatbuilders chapter were taken there. Kurt Nezbeda and I were graciously hosted by John Egan for a day at the Grumman History Center in Bethpage, NY. That was time very well spent.

I owe a great debt to my family who has supported me every step of the way and has been very forgiving about hearing stories of the good old days told over and over again. Special praise for my son Chris who guided me through the dark hole of online publishing. He also created the wonderful graphics for the book's front and back covers.

But most of all I owe great praise to my wife Cindy. How many times over the last three years has she heard me start a sentence with, "Did you know that…?," then listened to a soliloquy about some arcane piece of Amityville history. She never faltered from her unflagging support. She was also my first-line editor and compass—she never let me stray from the subject and was especially well-tuned to rooting out any BS or insensitive material.

The book is dedicated to the memory of my parents, Bob and Grace Robinson. It was their insightful decision to move the family to Ocean Avenue that made this all possible. They are a part of this book in so many ways.

INTRODUCTION

I was born and raised in Amityville, New York in the 1950s and '60s. It was a great time and place to grow up. My family moved off the Island during my college years and I never went back. My sons never got to know the town. After years of hearing my stories about growing up on the water, my sons persuaded me to write them down. The result was *My Amityville: Memories of a Golden Time*, self-published in 2015.

Writing the book tested my memory and I spent considerable time on research to get my facts straight. I began to see how Ocean Avenue fit into the history and development of Amityville and got to know the many famous, infamous and influential residents of Ocean Avenue in a new light. I remember sending an e-mail to John Bousquet, an Amityville friend, and talking about some of the information I had turned up, saying "I think there is another book in here somewhere." This is that book.

So, as it turns out, *The Golden Avenue: The History and People of Ocean Avenue, Amityville, NY*, is about 60% history, 40% biography and 5% autobiography, proving the great truism that the whole is greater than the sum of its parts. At least, I sincerely hope so.

A word about the title. That is a fifty-year-old gift from my wife, Cindy. We were dating in high school and she would often say, just to keep me in my place, "Oh, that's right, you live on the Golden Avenue." But, it really was!

CHAPTER 1: OCEAN AVENUE AND THE AMITYVILLE RIVER

Ocean Avenue starts at Merrick Road, in Amityville, and runs south for a mile or so, then makes a turn to the east ending at the village dock, looking out at the Great South Bay. Its most significant physical characteristic is that it runs parallel to the Amityville River which sits to the east about 100 yards, give or take. The history of the street is more aptly a history of the river because it is the river that gives Ocean Avenue its unique character. The river provided the water source for an early mill site, then was the avenue for early commerce, a desirable location for the hospitality industry beginning in the late nineteenth century, and finally an upscale residential location for families who wanted to be part of the Great South Bay boating community.

But the Amityville River isn't a river at all. It is, in fact, a tidal creek, which Wikipedia describes as "…the portion of a stream that is affected by ebb and flow of ocean tides, in the case that the subject stream discharges to an ocean, sea or strait." Ergo, the river is actually a creek and was properly called that up to the end of the nineteenth century. It can be confusing because the Amityville Creek has its beginning in North Amityville on the former Seth Platt Purdy farm, founded in 1781[1], and it ran south to Ireland's Pond (now Avon Lake), then under Merrick Road to become what we now call "the river." Up to, and

---

1   William T. Lauder, *Amityville History Revisited* (The Amityville Historical Society, 1992), 4

through, Ireland's Pond it was a stream, being fresh water without any tidal influence.

The humble creek appears to have become a river around the turn of the century at the time Ocean Avenue had just seen its first quarter-century wave of residential development of fine, large homes for the town's well-to-do citizens and summer visitors. Perhaps the residents felt their impressive homes deserved to back on something more grand than a simple creek, or crik as the old timers called it. For all my time living on Ocean Avenue it was the Amityville River so I will ignore historical correctness and continue the custom.

Merrick Road had its beginnings in pre-colonial days as an Indian trail running west to east, the full length of Long Island, from Brooklyn to Montauk Point. It runs along the island's southern shoreline, just touching the numerous bays, inlets, coves and creeks that give Long Island's south shore its "sawtooth" appearance. It was the most important east-west road in Long Island's early days and was the center of commercial traffic in early Amityville. Within two blocks of Ocean Avenue, Merrick Road saw the town's first public school, first church (the Methodist Episcopal Church) and most of the early businesses. Historical references can be confusing as Merrick Road had numerous names over time— South Road, South Turnpike, Montauk Highway, King's Highway and Main Street in Amityville.

The southernmost part of Amityville is made up of two "necks" or land areas that jut out into the bay. The appropriately named West Neck is bordered by the Narrasketuck Creek on the west and the Amityville River on the east. Josiah's Neck is adjacent to the east and bordered on its east side by Woods Creek. It was these two necks, south of Merrick Road, that were first deeded to white settlers by the Indians in 1658. In a further deed from the Indians in 1697, this land was confirmed in the names of John Ketcham, Jonas Platt, Timothy Conklin, Jr. and James Chichester,[2] most likely an ancestor of mine.

---

2   Lauder, 3

OCEAN AVENUE AND THE AMITYVILLE RIVER

This put the Amityville River and Ocean Avenue at the geographic center of the bay-centric early community. It would become the economic center of the early village as well.

However, the southern part of Amityville, south of Merrick Road, was most uninviting for residential living as it was mostly marshland infested with greenflies and mosquitoes. This was especially so for the southern half of Ocean Avenue which was primarily salt marsh, cattails and voracious mosquitoes. Before 1875 or so, Ocean Avenue was not much more than a dirt road providing access to the river for the baymen. In fact, it was first called the "Cow Path" as it led to the Ireland family meadow near the bay. It was later known as Ireland's Lane because so much of the land bordering the street was owned by the Ireland Family. It was mistakenly called Bayview Avenue on an 1873 map, and finally renamed Ocean Avenue because of the ferries that stopped at the village dock, at its foot, before running to the ocean beaches. Before Ocean Avenue was paved in 1922 the locals preferred to call it "Mud Lane."

Amityville was originally part of Huntington and called Huntington West Neck South or Huntington South West Neck.

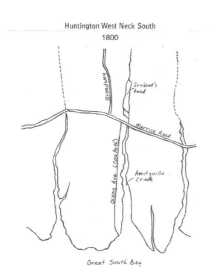

1.1 Huntington West Neck South, 1800

The "South" was necessary as there was already a village of West Neck in Huntington on the Long Island Sound. It was 1846 before the name change to Amityville was adopted. The area was first settled in the mid-1600s by English settlers moving south from the village of Huntington, Long Island. The southern length of Long Island was less desirable for farming because the soil was sandier and less fertile, but the bay and wetlands offered a bounty of fish, clams and oysters

1.2 An early twentieth century postcard view of Ireland's Mill looking north from Merrick Road.

as well as the naturally growing salt hay. Salt hay, or salt meadow cordgrass (*spartina patens*), is native to the Atlantic coastal wetlands and grew in great abundance in the marshes of the Great South Bay. It is unique in its ability to exude salt and thus thrive in saltwater meadows. The exuded salt made the salt hay a desirable feed for horses and cattle that needed a source of salt in their diets. The inventive settlers found other uses for the dried salt hay such as furniture stuffing, bedding, house insulation and garden mulch.

In 1750 Eliphalet Oakley established a sawmill on the west bank of the pond formed by the Amityville Creek just north of the South Road, now Merrick Road. He would sell the mill and property to his brother-in-law, Thomas Ireland, in 1793 when the pond became known as Ireland's Pond. Ireland added a grist mill on the southern end of the pond and the family operated the mills until 1880. This was an ideal site for the mills as the Amityville River provided access and egress for both mill inputs and finished products. This established the river as a central route for the transportation of milled grains, coal, lumber and the many commodities required by the growing community. The Irelands also ran a tavern and bakery at this location. The family became substantial investors in land on the yet-to-be-developed Ocean Avenue and were the first to build residences at the very top of Ocean Avenue, across the street from the mill property.

In 1846 the town name was changed from the cumbersome but descriptive Huntington West Neck South to Amityville. The more believable story behind the name choice has it that the town was named for John Ireland's boat the *Amity*. This would not be surprising. The Ireland family was one of the most prosperous in town with the *Amity* representing a significant source of the early commercial prosperity.

So, Ocean Avenue's beginning was humble at best. But the river it shadowed and serviced would host the Ireland Mill at its head and the village dock at its foot and provide access to the Great South Bay, the giver of life and industry to this colonial settlement. The story of Ocean Avenue is truly the story of how the town evolved and the people who shaped that change.

1.3 This early 1900s postcard shows Ocean Avenue looking south from about midway to the bay.

Chapter 2: A Little Long Island History

It helps to understand the development of Amityville by knowing the people who first settled there and the environment they both created and enjoyed.

Robert Caro, in his Pulitzer Prize winning biography, *The Power Broker: Robert Moses and The Fall of New York*, characterized the Great South Bay and its inhabitants as Robert Moses would have seen them in the early 1920s as he put his grand vision for Long Island into motion:

> *The Island's South Shore, the edge of the meadow that had been trans-*
> *formed into the Great South Bay, offered gentle waves and sandy*
> *beaches. But the bay was the haunt of the baymen, a closemouthed,*
> *independent breed, some of them descendants of families that had*
> *"followed the bay" since the Revolution, other New England Yankees*
> *who, hearing about the bay's bountiful harvests of oysters and clams,*
> *tomcods and smelts, had left the whaling boats and had moved to Long*
> *Island, bringing with them their taciturnity and distrust of outsiders.*

From the beginning of European settlement, Long Island was a prize much desired by the Dutch and the English. By virtue of Henry Hudson's original voyage for the Dutch

A LITTLE LONG ISLAND HISTORY

East India Company[1] in 1609, the Dutch were first to settle on Manhattan Island in the persons of Adrian Block and Audrick Christiance. They established a fort and settlement on Manhattan Island along with a fort in Albany, up the North (Hudson) River, to support a fur trading business.

But the English also felt they had claims to the new territory based on Sebastian Cabot's 1606 sail-by. It doesn't appear that Cabot spent any time in the area but his voyage gave the English some reason to argue their case. The Dutch controlled New Amsterdam (New York), New Jersey and Western Long Island while the English claimed New England and Eastern Long Island. They each encouraged settlement to reinforce their claims.

The early years were uneventful with a mixing of English and Dutch settlements in western Long Island. The Dutch settlers were traders and not overly concerned with government and control. The English settlers were anxious for religious freedom and self rule, and although they were technically under Dutch rule they were granted nearly complete autonomy with some formal oversight, mainly in choosing magistrates.

The English settlements on eastern Long Island had no political alliances and created their own governance which can be categorized as "pure democracy." [2] These settlements, including the West Neck area in South Huntington, had largely been populated by English immigrants from New England, first moving westward in Connecticut then across the Long Island Sound to Huntington then southward and eastward on Long Island. Although they may have had no political allegiances, they more closely aligned with the English settlements in Connecticut than the Dutch in New Amsterdam.

In 1650 the local Dutch and English authorities divided Long Island by a line running

---

1   Hudson was a British citizen sailing for the Dutch East India Company.

2   Benjamin F. Thompson, *The History of Long Island From Its Discovery And Settlement To The Present Time*, Volume 1 (first published in 1843, reprint 2015, Facsimile Printer 103 DDA Market Ashok Viher, Phase 3, Delhi, India), 109.

south from the Oyster Bay/Huntington town line to Fort Neck (Massapequa today) on the south shore, with the Dutch in control of the western part and the English the eastern part. This line is, essentially, the current Nassau/Suffolk county line.

By 1664 "The Dutch government, by its continued oppressions, had become generally unpopular; so much so, that even the Dutch inhabitants were greatly disgusted with the administration, and so the English were, of course, extremely anxious for a change."[3] The English towns were prepared to remove themselves from Dutch rule and had met over the winter and agreed to put themselves under Connecticut's rule. Interestingly, one of the issues the English settlers had with the Dutch was their treatment of the local Indians, which was often harsh and demeaning.

In this same year, in an effort to finally settle the dispute over Long Island, King Charles II, brother to James, Duke of York and Albany[4], granted James New Amsterdam, the name changed to New York, and Long Island. An invasion was planned to take these territories by force, if necessary, but Peter Stuyvesant, the Dutch Governor, wisely surrendered at the sight of the overwhelming English flotilla in the harbor.

But the new rule under the Duke of York was not idyllic. All of the freedoms the settlers had enjoyed were taken away. "The Duke's laws making no provision for a general assembly. The people had no voice in the government; but the governor had unlimited power, executive, legislative and judicial. He was commander-in-chief; all public officers were appointed by him, and most of them had their offices at his pleasure. With the advice of the council, he could make what laws he pleased, and could repeal them, even against the opinion or consent of the council."[5]

So the English colonists were once again in the position of being deprived of their

3   Ibid., 116

4   Upon his brother's death, James assumed the throne.

5   Thompson, 118

rights. Under English law citizens were assured of no taxation without representation, "… the power of disposing of his own money was the birthright of every British subject, and one of the elementary principles of British liberty…"[6] This would continue for eight years until the Dutch moved to retake control of New York and Long Island.

Starting in 1672 the Dutch sent out a naval force to destroy the English shipping channels in the Caribbean and up the coast of North America. In the process they captured 120 English and French merchant vessels. They then sailed into New York harbor in 1673 and took Manhattan without firing a shot. Thompson summed it up nicely, "The country which had now been nine years governed by the Duke of York's deputies, and experienced in very full measure the ill effects of ignorance and indiscretion in the conduct of its rulers, came once more under the government of their ancient masters, the Dutch."[7]

The Dutch wasted no time in reinstating their past magistrates and administrators and sending out a proclamation to all Long Island towns to send representatives and frame an oath of allegiance to the new Dutch governor. The eastern Long Island towns were somewhat reluctant to agree although they might fare better under Dutch rule than the previous nine years under the Duke of York. The town of Huntington responded in the positive with the stipulation they would not be required to take up arms against the English. This was quickly accepted by the Dutch.

Obviously this was not the end of the tug of war over Long Island. The following year, October 31,1674, with the signing of the Treaty of Westminster between the Dutch and the English, New York and Long Island were restored to English rule. But the English towns of eastern Long Island sought to align themselves with Connecticut to avoid going back under the harsh rule of the Duke of York. In a stunning display of open-mindedness, the Duke appealed to William Penn for advice on how to proceed with the feisty Long

---

6   Thompson, 147

7   Thompson, 150

Islanders. Penn's council was consistent with how he governed Pennsylvania- give the people the ability to self-govern. Thompson summed it up nicely: "At length, then, after long and unwearied efforts, on the 17th Oct., 1683, almost sixty years from the time the island of Manhattan was first occupied by a civilized people, and thirty years after the popular demand thereof, the representatives of the people met, and their self-established *charter of liberties* gave New York a place by the side of Virginia and Massachusetts. And thus, by the persuasions of a Quaker, (once so odious,) did a bigoted Roman catholic prince give orders to a popistical (sic) governor, to introduce a popular assembly, elected by the people themselves, and who had before no share in the government. An event similar in principle, and of nearly equal importance to the glorious independence which their descendants procured for themselves in less than a century after."[8]

But, as we know, in nearly a century's time, the issue of abrogation of inalienable rights would rear its ugly head again and the people of Long Island, as well as the rest of colonial America, would rise up against that tyranny.

* *

Thompson describes the town of Huntington in 1843 thusly, "Is bounded N. by the Sound, E. by a line running from French Pond to the N.W. angle of Winnecomak Patent; from thence down the creek E. of Sunquam's Neck, then down said creek to the South Bay, and then S. to a monument on the beach, fixed by commissioners in the year 1797; having Smithtown and Islip on the E. and Oyster Bay, Queen's County on the W... Its extent on the sound is about ten miles and upon the Bay six miles, and from N. to S. twenty miles."[9] [10]

---

8   Thompson, 161

9   Thompson, 465

10   An 1857 map showed an inlet at Gilgo Beach separating Jones Island from Oak Island with another inlet about where Hemlock Beach was in 1900. The town of Huntington included just the Oak Island section

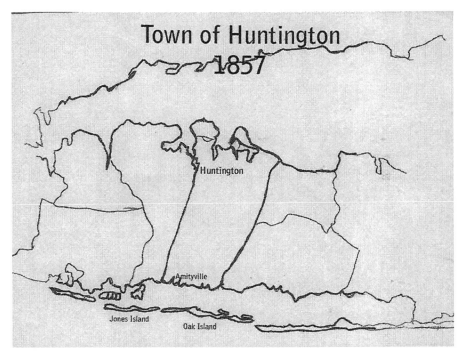

2.1 Town of Huntington, 1857

The first white settlers were fairly welcomed by the local Indians. The Long Island Indians were tributary to the Six Nations, the largest tribe and most feared being the Mohawks living along the Hudson River up into the north country. The Pequots, or Pequods, inhabited the Connecticut shore and would routinely raid eastern Long Island and exact tribute from the Indians there. It appears that the early Dutch settlers took over the dominant position held by the Mohawks and Pequots, along with the tribute they received, but offered some protection against further raids in return.

---

of the beach. These inlets did not exist into the 20th Century and the entire barrier island was technically Jones Island.

The Indian currency was wampum, a bead made from the local clam shells. The ability to create these black and white beads fell entirely to the Long Island tribes so the tributary relationship was significant in the native monetary system and continued into colonial times. The tribute exacted, first by the dominant tribes and then by the Dutch and English, was in wampum. This currency was so important to the early commerce of the area that the value of wampum was tied to the Dutch guilder and the British pound and established by legislation. Land purchased from the Indians was carefully monitored and done through a series of deeds, in writing, and filed with the authority in power at the time. That said, the value of land was insignificant by today's standards with typical payments from the settlers to the Indians of "blankets, clothing, fishing implements, and sometimes of guns and ammunition with a small quantity of wampum."[11] The Indians were only too happy to sell off this swampy, uninviting land because they had no concept of ownership. To them it just meant the land would be shared, as it had been for centuries.

The first property deeded to the white settlers in Huntington South was in 1654 for the two necks that are now Amityville, south of the Merrick Road. This deed was signed by Wyandance, the great sachem of the Massapequas. This was further defined in the deed of 1697, for the area known as West Neck, mentioned earlier.

In retrospect, it should have been surprising to those of us who grew up on Long Island, an area so rich with Indian town names, that there was scant Indian history and almost no remaining indigenous population. Thompson raises that issue in his 1843 *History of Long Island* and quotes Denton's 1670 history of New York, "There is now but few Indians, and these few no ways hurtful, but rather serviceable to the English; and it is to be admired, how strongly they have decreased, by the hand of God, since the English first settling in these parts. For, since my time (says he,) where there were six towns, they are reduced to two small villages; and it hath been generally observed, that where the

---

11   Thompson, 456

English came to settle, a *Divine Hand* makes way for them by *removing* or *cutting off* the Indians; other by wars, one with another, or by some mortal disease."[12] And this was as of 1670! While Denton attributes the (convenient?) decline in Indian population to a Divine Hand, there was nothing divine about continued infighting and the Indians' lack of natural resistance to European diseases. And look how quickly after the arrival of the white man that it happened.

We note some historical reference to Indian teepees on the outskirts of Amityville village in the mid-nineteenth century but no definable population exists there today. Many of the Long Island Indian tribes were very dark skinned and we know there was some intermarriage with the free black population which is one more factor that helps explain how such a once significant culture could disappear in just a few lifetimes.

---

12   Thompson, 80

Chapter 3- The Boat Builders of Ocean Avenue

Residential development of Ocean Avenue in the 19th Century was slow to start, with the commercial function of the river dominating its early history. With the river providing transportation for the Ireland's mills it is obvious that the availability of boats was essential for the success of that early commerce. The importance of these boats to the town's development helps explain why the Ireland family schooner, the *Amity*, was chosen as the namesake of the newly named village in 1846.[1]

The Irelands would be the first of the significant boat builders of Ocean Avenue, not as an occupation but as a necessary adjunct to their milling business. Before the arrival of boat builders by trade, the early merchants were forced to design and build boats to fit their specific needs. With the early focus of commerce on fishing, oystering, clamming and the harvesting of salt hay, a great variety of craft was required by the baymen.

The river activity reached a crescendo toward the end of the century and we see the emergence of the more well known Ocean Avenue boat builders. John K. Heinley established his coal business on Ocean Avenue around 1890. His business model was to source coal from the New York City area by boat and distribute it by wagon, locally, and by boat to towns on the Great South Bay. This required substantial vessels not available

---

1   The common legend claims the name was suggested during a rowdy and disruptive town meeting. A nice story but not likely.

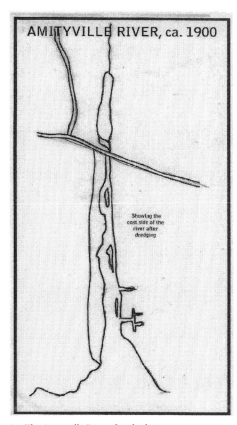

AMITYVILLE RIVER, ca. 1900

Showing the
east side of the
river after
dredging

3.1 The Amityville River after dredging.

locally so he added boat building to his curriculum vitae.

The first record of a Heinley built boat comes from the publication *Merchant Steam Vessels of the U.S.* of 1914 which lists the *J & C Heinley*, a 41-ton schooner built in 1892 in Amityville. She was 67 feet in length, 20.6 feet at the beam, with a draft of 4.8 feet and carrying a crew of two. This was a very substantial craft for the shallow waters of the Bay. Not dredged, the west end of the Bay was only four to six feet deep so drawing almost five feet could be a real problem.

It was about this time (1892), and likely connected, that the Amityville River was cut and dredged. A map of Amityville from 1888 shows the Amityville River meandering south from its beginning at Merrick Road with no real force to its flow to create or maintain any great depth. The shallowness of the Bay notwithstanding, the *J & C Heinley* would be hard pressed to make it out of the river except at high tide. But the River was not just dredged, it was dug along the eastern shore as well. A view of the River today shows the western shore as natural and winding as God made it but the eastern shore is straight as an arrow, as man re-made it. This significant achievement not only created a channel along the eastern shore of the river but also created three islands- Island #1 was in sight of Merrick Road (Enoch Island today), Island #2, across

3.2 The Amityville River, east bank, looking south. Island #2 is on the right and "Our Island" is straight ahead. Note the straight shore line of the east bank.

from Heinley's property on the west side of the River and a very small island further downstream that was insignificant enough that it was never given a name. (That island was across from our Ocean Avenue house so we called it "Our Island")

With the river then capable of accommodating the sizable craft necessary for transporting coal in and out, Heinley set about building a fleet of boats for his business. He is credited with building the *Elizabeth Befell*, a 37-footer, the *Bay Queen*, a fifty-two footer and the *J. Clark Curtain*, a schooner[2] (two masted) built later for his neighbor "Ruck" Wicks whose brother Frank Wicks, at that time, was a boat builder and next door neighbor to the north. Ruck skippered the *J. Clark Curtin* as a ferry to the ocean beaches.

---

2   Niemi, Victoria, *Boat Building in Amityville*: (The Department of History, Stony Brook University, Fall 2002/Spring 2003), n.p,

Frank Wicks located his boat building business at 152 Ocean Avenue, just north of Heinley's coal tower. We first see reference to a Wicks built boat in the 1896 American Yacht List. It shows the *White Wings* under "Sail Yachts", a cat boat designed and built by Frank Wicks and owned by Bernard Kortright of Amityville. Wicks, along with his three sons, developed a business of designing and building high quality small to large sailing craft. His boats were known to be not only beautiful and well made but easy to handle and very seaworthy.

The most iconic of Wicks' boats was the *Commodore*, built in 1913 and described by Amityville historian Bill Lauder as a "...shallow draft Great South Bay schooner." This from Lauder's 2005

3.3 The Commodore berthed on the Narrasketuck Creek, Amityville, ca. 1977. Photo Courtesy Kurt Nezbeda

Eulogy For The Commodore which tells the story of one of the "...finest sailing yachts ever to grace Long Island's South Shore."[3]

The *Commodore* was built for John Vanderveer with the instruction to "spare no expense." She was registered as 40-feet at the waterline and 72-feet in length from the tip of the 12-foot bow sprit to the butt of the 6-foot boomkin which extended off the stern. She had an ample beam of 15+ feet and was designed specifically to sail the shallow

---

3   Lauder, William T., *Eulogy for the Commodore*, (Historical Supplement to the Amityville Historical Society Dispatch) n.p.

waters of the west end of the Great South Bay. Originally designed as a sloop, she had a single 55-foot mast with a Marconi (triangular) mainsail and jib. She was later converted to a schooner, with two masts, the aft mast being the taller of the two. Under full sail she carried 1100 square feet of sail and was a beautiful sight to see.

The *Commodore* changed hands a few times, then in 1953 Gil Haight bought her and brought her back to the Amityville River, just a stone's skip from where she was built. We had just moved back to Amityville in 1953 and the *Commodore* was berthed a few houses north of us on the west bank of the river. As a young boy I marveled at her beautiful lines and elegant design. Gathering up all my courage I once climbed the rigging to sit on the crows nest nearly atop the 55-foot mast. The view from there was spectacular. At Christmastime Haight would hoist a Christmas tree and lights to the top of the mast

3.4 The Nezbedas and friends aboard the *Falcon* on the Wilmington River in Savannah, Georgia ca. 1978. Photo courtesy Kurt Nezbeda

3.5 The Wicks picnic style boat, *Sea Change*, built in 1929. Photo courtesy Barth Keller

and it could be seen for miles. Sadly, Bill Lauder's article was, indeed, a eulogy for the *Commodore*- past her prime and lacking someone to make the investment to put her back in seaworthy condition she was cut up in 2006.

My good friend Kurt Nezbeda bought a Wicks sloop and took it with him when his work with Grumman took him to Savannah, Georgia. The boat was the *Falcon*, built by the Wicks Brothers in 1938 for a local Amityville customer. She had the same classic lines as the *Commodore* and was made with the same quality craftsmanship. The Wicks Brothers used full length, long-leaf pine planks over an oak frame resulting in a hull that was almost free of leakage, even after years of service. The old timers talked of the extra long planks coming into Amityville by rail then trucked to the boat yard where they were submerged in the river for a year before they were ready for construction.

Nezbeda took the *Falcon* down to Savannah through the inland waterway in 1978 and he uses the word "interesting" to describe the trip which included a failed "head" and nagging engine trouble. A later bachelor party aboard the boat with 20 U.S. Army Rangers and a keg of beer added to the *Falcon* lore.

Wicks ran the business with his sons Oliver, Clifford and William. Starting in the late 1920s, following their father's death, the brothers ran the boatyard and were prolific builders of power and sail boats through 1949. They are credited with building 90 "picnic-style" power boats from 1930 to 1940. The picnic-style boat was typically from 30 to 40 feet long with a raised cabin and covered cockpit in the stern. These were very popular cruising boats on the bay and the Long Island Sound. John Vanderveer so loved the *Commodore* he had the Wicks Brothers build two of these picnic-boats for him, the *Jay Vee* in 1931 (31-feet) and a larger, 37-foot version in 1937 christened the *Jay Vee II*[4]. The *Sea Change*, pictured here, was owned by the Kellers and docked at their 278 Ocean Avenue home for much of the later part of the last century.

The third significant Ocean Avenue name in boat building was Ketcham, two cousins, in fact, Wilbur and Paul. Wilbur made a grand statement in the business in 1935 with the introduction of the Narrasketuck, single class, center-board sloop. The Narrasketuck Yacht Club had just formed in 1933 and was looking for a single class boat, suitable for the shallow Great South Bay and easy enough to build that a large, competitive class could be created. Ketcham's 20' 6" centerboard sloop was selected and the Narrasketuck was born.[5] Ketcham kept the freeboard low and design sleek, with a nearly flat bottom, center board, healthy beam, mainsail and jib. He succeeded in designing the perfect competitive racer for the local waters.

From Wilbur's boathouse and shop on Island #2 in the Amityville River came the

---

4   WoodenBoat Magazine/Resources/Register of Wooden Boats/Charlie, posted 12/31/2013

5   The Narrasketuck was named for the sponsoring Yacht Club which was named for the creek that forms the western boundary of Amityville on its south shore. The early site for the Narrasketuck Yacht Club meetings was Island #1 in the Amityville River but it was fittingly relocated to the banks of the Narrasketuck Creek in the 1950s.

Narrasketuck

L.O.A. 20' 6"
BEAM 6' 6"
DRAFT 1' 0"
DRAFT C.B. DOWN 3' 0"

3.6 The Narrasketuck one-design

first 7 Narrasketucks, the first six for sale to anxious sailors[6] but number seven (his lucky number) he kept for himself. He named it *Defiance* and painted it a powder blue. Old #7 would become an iconic sight on the Great South Bay. On race days I can remember watching Wilbur tack his #7 past our house and out to the bay. Our shouted greetings always met with a warm smile and a wave.

Wilbur lived on Ocean Avenue a few houses south of the Wicks and Heinley properties but his boatyard was the south half of Island #2. He rowed to work every day, a fitting start for a boat builder and bayman. At its peak the property boasted seven sets of rails for hauling boats out of the water, for outside work or inside his shop, and a one-lung gas engine to power the winch for the rail cars. During the wooden boat years this was the preferred way to move the boats and each of the Ocean Avenue boatyards had at least one rail line. The Heinley property boasted a set of rails and a capstan[7] to move the large boats he was building.

In the late '30s other local boat builders joined Wilbur in building up the fleet and by the 1950s the Narrasketuck became the largest single class to compete at regattas on the

---

6   Narrasketuck #6 was purchased by Robert Moses, of Babylon, L.I., for his daughter, Jane. Moses was already on his way to becoming the most powerful New York State politician , a distinction he would hold for four decades without ever holding elected office. In 1947 Ketcham built Jane Moses Collins her second Narrasketuck, #55.

7   The capstan was a horizontal wheel where livestock were hitched to provide power for the winch.

3.7 Wilbur Ketcham's #7 *Defiance* on display at the Long Island Maritime Museum.

bay, a fleet of 150 boats. Wilbur focused his boat building on non-powered, small sailing craft. It was during this time that the Amityville River had moved from a commercial waterway to a residential back yard. Wooden boats for fun and sport were the new order of the day and he worked the transition well. A nice example of an early Wilbur Ketcham cat boat is the *Yes Pop*, one of two W-Cats owned by John Hearns. The Hearns family lived a few houses south of us on Ocean Avenue. The *Yes Pop* is cited in the 1974 history of the Narrasketuck Yacht Club as the only boat in the club to be owned and sailed by a single owner (John Hearns) for the 40 years the club had been in existence. The sister Ketcham W-cat, the *So Long*, was retired by Hearns and now resides at the Long Island Maritime Museum in Sayville, Long Island.

Wilbur did abandon his "sail only" philosophy to make a few "stink pots," the *Pilgrim*, owned by John Hearns, being one of at least three to his credit. In my day the handsome cabin cruiser was docked behind the Hearns family home on Ocean Avenue and was a familiar sight on the bay.

When not building boats Wilbur was skippering *Defiance* in one race or another. He

3.8 A happy Bucky Parker sails the Yes Pop with a bevy of beauties, ca. 1966. Photo courtesy Charles (Bucky) Parker

3.9 The Pilgrim during Race Week, 1971. Photo courtesy Charles (Bucky) Parker

was a great competitor and capped his long, successful career by winning the Queen of the Bay regatta for the second time in 1961 just shy of his 79th birthday. He won it the first time in 1949.

In September of 2015 I had the pleasure of spending an afternoon with Owen Brooks, my early sailing mentor and a senior and esteemed member of the Great South Bay sailing community. Owen lived on Riverside Drive on the east bank of the Amityville River, with his boat house about even with Wilbur Ketcham's shop on Island #2. People loved to tell Wilbur Ketcham stories and Owen related this one to me. He first asked if I knew that Wilbur was a sailmaker as well as a boat builder, and I had to admit I did not. It seems that shortly after Wilbur won the Queen of the Bay title in 1961 he was showing a fellow "salt" a picture of the *Defiance* crossing the finish line of the deciding race. Wilbur had made the suit of sails used that day out of a powder blue nylon to coordinate with the hull color of *Defiance*. The non-traditional material had gotten wet and stretched to the point the sails looked almost comical, but not funny to someone as serious about the sport as Wilbur. And to make the critical point, Wilbur pointed to a boat in the picture, a mere trailing speck, and said "That's the guy who came in second." Enough said about baggy sails!

Wilbur's cousin, Paul, also created an iconic sailboat to Amityville. The Great South Bay had a strong past in the design and production of working boats for the baymen. One common design was a "gunning" boat commonly used by market hunters, sport hunters and baymen as a utility craft. They were around 14 feet long, round bottomed with a single sprit-rigged sail and centerboard. Each varied a little depending on the maker. They could

3.10 Seaford Skiff #1 on display at the Long Island Maritime Museum.

be sailed, rowed, poled or pulled over the ice. Built of oak and cedar they were almost indestructible, a good quality for boats that took a beating by their very nature.

Legend has it that in 1944 Frank Rau asked Paul if he could make one of these skiffs for him and Paul said, yes, if he had one to go by. Frank got hold of Walter Ashdown who owned a Seaford Skiff built in 1880 by Will Gritman and Paul used that as his model.[8] Ketcham built the first one for Ashdown then made #1 for Frank Rau. They became extremely popular in Amityville and neighboring towns along the bay as training boats for young sailors. They had all the requisites- indestructible, easy to sail, almost impossible to flip and easy to pull out of the water. They also doubled as a great duck boat for dad in the winter. By 1963 Paul Ketcham, with the help of his wife and Paul, Jr., had built 50 Seaford Skiffs.

---

8   Humbert O. Martin, *The Seaford Skiff*, (The Amityville Record, Amityville, NY), date unknown.

THE BOAT BUILDERS OF OCEAN AVENUE

Barry Thomas was almost poetic as he wrote about building a skiff for his 10-year old son:

> *The little skiff is restless at her mooring. She is round bottomed, about*
> *fourteen feet, and decked over but for a small cockpit. Her spritsail and*
> *boom are lashed to the mast. Once aboard, it takes but a minute to*
> *unleash the boom and sail, grab the grout in the madly flailing peak,*
> *insert the sprit end therein and hoist it aloft, pass the snotter through the*
> *hole in the lower sprit and set it up with a rolling hitch on the sprit, ram*
> *the tiller into the rudder head, cast off the mooring and sheet her in.*[9]

The Mellon Seed and Paul Ketcham's Seaford Skiff share a common, general design and misty heritage. Built from the late 1800s until the age of the baymen came to a close in the early 1900s, the style was saved by the efforts of Paul Ketcham and others like him who didn't want to see the design fade into obscurity.

Owen Brooks remembered some of the early Seaford Skiff sailors- Randy Ronback whose father ran his business of dock building and dredging directly across the river from our house, and Myton Ireland, who would much later be our neighbor one lot to the north on the river. Peter and Terry O'Malley[10], the son and daughter of Walter O'Malley of Brooklyn Dodger ownership fame, sailed #10 from their home at 318 Ocean Avenue and right next door, the Nezbedas, sailed #2. #1 was eventually retired and currently resides at the Long Island Maritime Museum in Sayville, Long Island.

I was told a story, long, long ago that captures the essence of the two boats by the Ketcham cousins. It is said that on a Saturday race day, off the Amityville shore, the fleet of Narrasketucks heading for the leeward mark were overtaking the Seaford Skiffs. It helps to understand that the boat classes were started in order of their speed- the Narrasketuks, the fastest, always went first and the Seaford Skiffs, the slowest, always last. This so the faster

---

9   Barry Thomas, *The Mellon Seed and the Seaford Skiff*, (The Log of Mystic Seaport, Volume 26, Number 2, Summer 1974)

10   Terry O'Malley would later sail her *Blizzard*, Narrasketuck #88, with great success.

classes didn't have to sail through the slower boats. To compensate for their speed the Narrasketucks sailed the course twice and on this day they had lapped the pokey Seaford Skiffs on their second leeward leg. For the non-sailing reader the leeward mark was the end of the downwind leg of the race and rounding the mark required a "jibe" which is the trickiest maneuver a sail boat makes and requires significant skills, especially with sophisticated racing craft such as the Narrasketuck.

So the Narrasketucks, sailed by veteran, steely-eyed men, were lapping the Seaford Skiffs right at the mark. The 'Tuck skippers were too arrogant to give way to a bunch of kids and the Skiff skippers (10-year olds mostly) weren't smart enough to get out of their way. The result was a hellish conflagration at the mark with none giving ground and the 10-year olds learning new words from men they knew better from Sunday school class. In the end, what the spectators saw was one 'Tuck flip over and another break its mast, but the lowly Seaford Skiffs, unscathed, calmly sailed on to finish the race.

The Paul Ketcham family boat business lived on with Paul Jr. running it from the shop on New Point Creek, a block or so east of the Amityville river. He started working with his dad in 1958 and bought the business from him in 1991. But the demise of the wooden boat in favor of maintenance-free fiberglass has reduced the demand for the traditional woodworking skills of craftsmen such as Paul Ketcham.

In 2015 the Amityville Record posed an open question to its readers, "What do you love about your hometown?" Owen Brooks sent in the following which was published in the August 31, 2015, edition:

> Back in the late 1970's, my son and I raced our Hereshoff 12 1/2
> in the Babylon Yacht Club Annual July 4 Weekend Regatta. The
> final race was cancelled because of high winds. Therefore, Jon and
> I sailed our small boat out in the bay and started the long wet
> beat against the wind to Amityville. Off Lindenhurst, the lower
> pintle broke off the rudder just below the upper pintle and disap-

peared forever. We ultimately made it home steering with an oar.

*As soon as I got home, I headed for Paul Ketcham's Boatyard on New
Point Place to see if "Old Paul" would make a new five-and-one-half-foot-
long rudder for a 1914 designed boat. He said he would if I gave him the
dimensions and fittings. Each day after work, on the way home from the
LIRR, I'd stop by the yard to view the progress. One day when I thought he
should be about finished, I stopped by, but he wasn't there.
The shop was open, so I looked around for the rudder but couldn't find
it. Muriel, Paul's wife, must have heard me and started down the inside
stairs. When she saw me, she said with relief, "Oh, it's you! Paul went to the
barber." She said that Paul knew I was so finicky and didn't want anything
to happen to the rudder, so it was up in the bed. I asked where they were
going to sleep and she said the rudder was on the guest bed. Where else can
you get that kind of friendly boatyard service except in the Friendly Village?*

*We won a lot more races with the new rudder and Paul's
beautiful handiwork is still on the stern of "Target," now renamed
"Minx," on display in the Hall of Boats in the Hereshoff Marine
Museum at Bristol, Rhode Island where she was built.*

It seems a bit ironic today that the three best known boat builders of Amityville-John
Heinley, Frank Wicks and Wilbur Ketcham- were not only from the same river and street,
but they had three adjacent properties, all on the east side of Ocean Avenue. In 1973 Steve
Brice, an electrical engineer by education, bought the boatyard at 144 Ocean Avenue from
Bob Schwarzler but better known in my day as Jim's Boatyard. The property had a long
history of boat builders including owners Puggy Melick and Bill Conlin, an early skipper
of one of the iconic ocean beach ferry boats sailing out of the Amityville River. That site
had been joined with the property at 152 Ocean Avenue, formerly the Wicks Boatyard.
Steve would later double the size of his empire by adding the adjacent lot, the former

Heinley property. All three of these boat yards sat behind turn-of-the-century homes sitting up on Ocean Avenue.

Steve was a boyhood friend, growing up a little south of us on Ocean Avenue. He jumped into the business after spending his youth as a bay rat and a few summers working at Jim's boatyard. His work at Grumman Aircraft was not rewarding and he longed to use his skills to build his own business, so he took the leap of faith.

And a leap it was. The small boat construction business was in the process of changing from a one-off construction in wood to an assembly line process in fiberglass. The 1960s had seen a mass migration to fiberglass and an end to wooden boat construction at the local boat yards. Many of the older boat owners doggedly fought the fiberglass temptation and kept the boat yards somewhat busy with repairs on their aging wooden boats, but as the "X" generation took to the water they did so in shiny fiberglass. The challenge for Steve and his son was to chart a course through these troubled waters that would develop a profitable, sustainable business, without the traditional work on wooden boats.

The recipe involved a transition from sales to service and sail to power, with the

3.11 Looking north along the west bank of the Amityville River, amidst the boat building properties. The Heinley coal tower sits proudly, if not elegantly, in the background.

modern day Yacht Service, Inc. providing a high value service package for high value power boaters. As of this writing Steve has sold the business to his son, Todd, effective in 2008. Steve worked part time just to keep at it a bit. The plan was to work just a few years, but it lasted to 2016 when Steve retired for good.

Sadly, from an historic perspective, Yacht Service, Inc. is the only surviving commercial entity on Ocean Avenue.

CHAPTER 4- FERRIES AND OCEAN BEACHES

The geography of early Huntington went, north to south, from the Long Island Sound to the Atlantic Ocean and included a significant portion of what was first called the South Beach and would technically become Jones Island. The south coast including the barrier island[1] and all the marshes in-between was the environment of Amityville baymen and a critical part of the town's commerce.

In those early days the commercial shipping lanes were closer to land than they are now and shipwrecks off Jones Island were a common occurrence. During the middle of the 19th Century the Federal Government set up a series of Life Saving Stations on the sections of the Atlantic coastline, from Maine to Florida, most at risk for shipwrecks. Because of the severity of the problem along Jones Island five stations were built, one each (west to east) at Short Beach, Zach's inlet, Jones Beach, Gilgo Beach, and Oak Island Beach, stretching the scant 20 miles from Zach's inlet to Fire Island inlet.

These stations were built to accommodate a crew of six or so for four to six weeks at a time. They would patrol the beach and lend assistance to any ships that found the shoals. Each crew would be spelled by a second crew so that constant watch could be kept. During the latter part of the 19th century small seasonal resort communities grew

---

1   An 1857 map of Long Island shows an inlet at Gilgo Beach separating the barrier island into two with Jones Island ending at that point, near the Nassau/Suffolk county line. The eastern part was called Oak Island. The inlet would later heal itself rejoining the two islands. For ease of description I will refer to the entire barrier island, from Zach's Bay to Fire Island, as Jones Island.

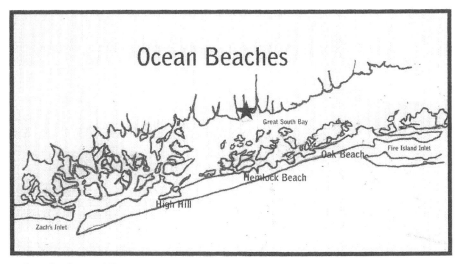

4.1 Ocean beaches ca. 1900

up around the life saving stations at most of their locations. By the late 1800s there were resort communities at Zach's Inlet (High Hill), Jones Beach (sometimes called High Hill), Hemlock Beach (Gilgo Beach) and Oak Island Beach (Oak Beach).[2] In 1915 the Life Saving Service was folded into the newly created Coast Guard and all but the Zach's Bay location were abandoned in favor of patrolling by water. The resort communities had grown to the point that the loss of the Life Saving Stations had little effect and they continued to be a favorite summer destination for the locals as well as a growing number of New York and Brooklyn vacationers.

The Amityville folks tended to favor Hemlock Beach and the emerging scheduled ferry service out of Amityville would favor this destination although High Hill and Oak Island Beaches were also serviced out of the Amityville River but on a non-scheduled

---

2   Lauder, 34

4.2 High Hill Beach looking Southwest from the
hotel, 1928

4.3 Wilmarth Pavilion at High Hill Beach

basis. Frank Wicks started running a boat to Hemlock Beach every Friday in 1875[3] as
the community had grown to have a few boarding houses and cottages for rent. Then
about 1883 Wesley VanNostrand built a pavilion there with food and beverages and
entertainment on Saturday nights. He included a substantial dock for the ferry boats
which encouraged greater traffic.

On an interesting note, High Hill was the most sophisticated ocean beach
development boasting its own central water supply, boarding house, post office and 70
cottages. Unfortunately for its summer residents and visitors, High Hill stood in the way
of Robert Moses' Jones Beach State Park development and in 1940 the land leases were not
renewed. Many of the cottages were moved to neighboring West Gilgo Beach and those
not moved were demolished. That land is now part of the Jones Beach complex.[4]

Until Jones Beach State Park was completed in 1929, the only access to the island
beaches was by water, so a system of ferry service was required and it is not surprising
that the boatbuilders of Ocean Avenue were front and center in this regard. The early
ferry service out of the Amityville River was unscheduled and provided by local baymen

---

3   Ibid, 35

4   Ibid, 35

4.4 Looking North to the ferry landing at the head of Ocean Avenue. On the other side of the bridge is Ireland's Pond. You can just see a portion of the Ireland home to the left. The mills are not visible in this photo. Postmarked 1921.

in their sail powered catboats. These were shallow draft, wide beam, single masted sloops favored for bay commerce for their reliable service in the shallow bay.

By 1871 we know of the *Davidson* sailing to Hemlock Beach and in 1882 Frank Wicks and Asa Chichester offered ferry service on their cat boats. 1888 saw William Ketcham offering the first steam ferry service to Hemlock Beach aboard the *W.J.*[5]

With the turn of the century we see the adoption of new technology and the first scheduled ferry service to the island beaches. In 1900 Charles Sprague ran his flat bottomed New

---

5   Ibid, 31

4.5 Wicks ad.

4.6 The pavilion at Hemlock Beach. Post marked 1911

4.7 The Columbia docked at the Hemlock Beach Pavilion. Post marked 1913.

Haven Sharpie, *Echo*, to and from Hemlock Beach. With the popularity of the island beaches growing rapidly, Frank Wicks modified his cat boat, the *W.L.V.*, in 1902 by splicing in an additional 6 feet of length, adding a second deck, a gasoline engine and side paddles, and launched what is believed to be the first regularly scheduled ferry service to Hemlock Beach. Frank Wick's brother "Ruck" skippered his *J. Clark Curtin* ferry to the islands as well.

In 1903 Charles Sprague built the 48-foot *Adel*, a flat-bottomed, gasoline powered side-wheeler, one of the "big three" gasoline powered ferries to sail out of the Amityville River. Sprague ran the *Adel* from a dock on the east side of the Amityville River, just south of the Merrick Road.

In 1905 Wicks added the *Atlantic* to his ferry fleet. At 52 feet and with gasoline screw propulsion, she carried 180 passengers and became the queen of the fleet. Wicks also operated the *Columbia* and was the most prominent ferry boat captain out of the Amityville River. A note in the "Personals" section of the Amityville Record, July 2, 1902, reads, "Steamer Columbia, Captain Frank Wicks, Leaves Wick's Dock daily for Hemlock Beach, Excursion fare 25 cts." At various times he would board passengers at his dock on

4.8 An early photo postcard, ca. 1910, of a ferry landing at the Oak Island Beach.

Ocean Avenue, at a dock on the west side of the river at Merrick Road[6] and also make a stop at the village dock at the foot of Ocean Avenue to take on passengers from the Cross-Island Trolley.[7] For a short time the lower portion of the "West Neck" was called "Ocean Point" because of the access to the ocean the ferries provided and the Ocean Point Hotel built on the water at the foot of Ocean Avenue. With the termination of trolley service to Amityville in 1920, the ferries went back to their previous loading docks up river near Merrick Road.

With Frank Wicks' death in 1921 the *Atlantic* and *Columbia* were sold to William G.

---

6   In its first year of operation in 1909 the cross island trolley terminated on Merrick Road at the head of the Amityville River. This became the best boarding location for trolley/ferry passengers. The trolley line was extended to the village dock at the foot of Ocean Avenue in 1910.

7   The cross-island trolley ran to the Amityville Village dock from 1910 to 1920.

Conley who had been their master under Wicks. Conley continued to operate both boats as scheduled ferry service.

This colorful age of ferries to ocean beach communities came to an abrupt end in the early 1930s. Robert Moses had completed his monumental Jones Beach State Park project in 1929. His vision for a Long Island state park complex revolved around a series of parkways (a term he invented) including today's Southern State Parkway, Robert Moses Parkway, Captree Bridge and Ocean Parkway, all necessary to complete the ring of parkways circling the western section of the Great South Bay.

Moses was confronted with the problem that the towns of Hempstead and Babylon had been granted rights to the bay and barrier island in 19th Century state legislation and they guarded those rights fiercely. Moses was able to complete the first, small, section of the Ocean Parkway, up to the Nassau/Suffolk County line, in 1929, with the completion of Jones Beach, by politically strong arming the Town of Hempstead. The town of Babylon held fast and refused to take the matter to the voters, as was necessary by law. It was quietly suggested to Moses that he have a conversation with Judge Hildreth of Amityville who, it was whispered, had some valuable information. Hildreth told Moses that, based on some earlier legal work he had done, it turned out the 19th century legislation giving the Town of Babylon the rights to the bay and barrier island had never passed.[8]

Moses then had a very frank meeting with the Babylon town supervisors and made them an offer they couldn't refuse. If they gave him the rights to build his road, he would make sure they had the rights to the bay bottom they sorely coveted. And Moses would do this without exposing the town's malfeasance to their constituents. It was quickly done.

Having the rights to build his road Moses set about first dredging the State Boat Channel from Zach's Bay to Fire Island Inlet. He sold this to the Babylon supervisors as a freebee but he needed the dredged material to raise the level of the island for his road bed. The raised road bed had the added benefit of precluding any future breaches of the island,

---

8   Caro, 235

a surprisingly common occurrence during the past century. This was done and Moses' parkway was completed by 1933. This provided access by automobile to all of the island beaches the entire length of Jones Island and, sadly, the more romantic and picturesque but less convenient ferry service became a thing of the past.

CHAPTER 5- THE GRAND HOTELS

Ultimately, the event that had the most impact on the development of Amityville and Ocean Avenue was the arrival of the Long Island Railroad in 1867.

Up until then Amityville was a quiet bay community with roots and ties to the English settlers who migrated from Massachusetts first to the central Connecticut coast then across the Long Island Sound to Huntington then south to what would become Amityville. Prior to the arrival of the railroad, the village, just 20 miles from Huntington, had familial ties to the English settlers there. By contrast, they were 35 miles from Brooklyn and New York which was an eleven hour stage coach ride plus a ferry ride if the destination was New York.[1]

The new rail line took that travel time from eleven hours to one hour for the same one dollar fare. The result was a dramatic increase in the movement of goods and people to and from Amityville. The population of South Huntington, including Amityville, tripled from the pre-Civil War number of about one thousand to three thousand after the war. The biggest drawing cards were the moderate temperatures and recreation afforded by the ocean and bay.

With easy access from New York and Brooklyn, the well kept secrets of the local recreation in Amityville were soon known to the world. With the ocean beaches, swimming, boating and fishing in summer and boating, fishing and hunting in Spring and

---

1   Lauder, 8

5.1 The Hotel New Point aka The South Shore Holiday House around 1910

Fall, Amityville became a prime destination for the well-to-do from the city.

The first of the grand, bay-side hotels, the Ocean Point Hotel, was built at the foot of Ocean Avenue in the 1880s. It offered great views of the bay and was adjacent to the village dock with access to fresh seafood from the fishing, clamming and oyster boats. The hotel likely offered boat rentals and organized excursions to the barrier island communities of High Point, Hemlock Beach and Oak Beach Island. Little information about the hotel survives; it burned to the ground around 1900 and was not rebuilt. In 1907 the Mortimer Palmer House was built on the property and remains today as an example of gracious, late Victorian architecture and a reminder of the Golden Age of Ocean Avenue development.

In 1892 John E. Ireland, of the founding Irelands and Ocean Avenue resident, developed the Hotel New Point which was considered the finest Long Island resort of its

HATHAWAY INN ON GREAT SOUTH BAY - AMITYVILLE, L. I., N. Y.

5.2 The Hathaway Inn, sister hotel to the New Point Hotel.

day. The hotel sat on the east bank of the mouth of the Amityville River with every guest room commanding a spectacular view of the bay. The imposing structure stood three and one half stories tall with sixty guest rooms. The hotel offered free carriage service to and from the Long Island Railway station in the village and boasted a carriage house and livery for those guests arriving in their own carriages.

Open from May to October the Hotel New Point treated its guests to the beauties of the Great South Bay from Spring to Fall. The hotel was so successful the New Point Inn was built in 1900 to handle the overflow from the hotel. It sat adjacent to the hotel on its western side offering the same view of the bay. In 1906 the name was changed to the Hathaway House.

The teens saw some softness in bookings and the hotel was remodeled and upgraded. An ad that ran in the *Sunday New York Tribune*, June 2, 1912, boasted "Bathing, Boating,

The Inn   Amityville, Long Island   Hotel New Point
                                              Ewen Hathaway
                                              Proprietor

5.3 The Hathaway Inn is to the left and the New Point Hotel to the right.

Fishing, Tennis" and "The Finest Sea Shore Resort Hotel on Long Island." Part of the ad copy read "The Hotel New Point, on the shore and overlooking Great South Bay has been entirely renovated. Billiard Room, Bowling Alleys, Cafe, Grill and many other luxuries that all help to make an enjoyable summer. Every room overlooks the bay. Rooms and rooms en suite with baths, electric light. The rooms are the largest and coolest of any hotel on Long Island."

Despite such irresistible prose the hotel was losing favor and was closed in 1916, its contents sold at auction. The Hathaway House continued in operation until 1951 when it burned to the ground, a common fate for the early wooden hotels in Amityville.

There are many stories about the guests at the Hotel New Point and Hathaway House, many of which revolve around members of the New York crime families, alcohol, boats and a lack of basic seamanship of those guests. The good news is that the "good fellas"

5.4 A nostalgic watercolor by Rudy Sittler, of the three principle Amityville River ferries, *Columbia*, *Atlantic* and *Adel* sailing by the Hotel New Point, prior to1900 when the Hathaway Inn was built. Photo courtesy Rudy Sittler, Jr.

were reasonably good citizens when on vacation, leaving their criminal activities back in the city. Amityville remained a safe place to live.

After closing, the Hotel New Point remained standing and the first floor was used as a fresh air camp for city youth for a while then as the Meroke Day Camp in the late 1950s. My older brother, Bob, was a sailing instructor there one summer. By 1960 it was boarded up and in 1962, you guessed it, it burned to the ground. Many of my friends watched the spectacular blaze from their boats out in the bay. Although the hotel was within sight from our sun

5.5 The Hotel New Point ablaze in 1962. Photo courtesy Thom Fleming.

FOOT OF OCEAN AVE ,AMITYVILLE ,N.Y.

5.6 A 1927 postcard view of the Mortimer Palmer House which sits on the site of the former Ocean Point Hotel. The photograph was taken looking north from the parking lot of the Narragansett Inn. The village dock is to the right.

porch I missed the whole thing.

The hotel had been the most commanding structure on the shore line and was a natural beacon in the mouth of the Amityville River. It had provided bearings and steered many a weary sailor home in good weather and bad. It was missed.

The third of the big three bay front hotels was the Narragansett, built at the foot of Ocean Avenue across the street from where the Ocean Point Hotel had stood and adjacent to the village dock. Originally called the Conklin House for its owner, Bernie Conklin, the hotel and restaurant looked out at the bay and had a great view of the Hathaway House and Hotel New Point, just across the mouth of the Amityville River. Conklin was a good promoter and arranged excursions and boat trips for his guests. William Conley operated

Old Narragansett Inn, Amityville, L. I.

5.7 The Narragansett Inn from a post card likely in the early 1920s when it was called Shanahans. The village dock is just outside the photo to the left.

his *Ella C.* and Josh Burch sailed the *Barney Conklin* from the hotel dock.[2] From 1910 to 1920 the cross island ferry terminated next door at the village dock and must have been a real plus for guests arriving by train.

Conklin also operated a beach on the property which was likely the first public beach in the village. Details are a little sketchy but Dennis O'Brien also ran a public beach adjacent to the Narragansett property in the 1910s and '20s. The locations for these two beaches is logical realizing the trolley provided easy access from 1910 to 1920.

During the Prohibition years the Narragansett was sold and operated as a restaurant under the new name, Shanahans. It was later sold again with another name change to Shangri-La and operated as a bar and restaurant. Completing the almost required end to all Amityville resort hotels the Narragansett, aka Shanihans, aka Shangri-La, succumbed

---

2   Karen Mormando Klein, *Amityville*, (Arcadia Publishing, 2012), 57

to a kitchen fire in 1965 and was razed. Today, the site has residential homes replacing the hotel.

CHAPTER 6- THE YACHT CLUB AND THE END OF THE BEGINNING

The coming of the railroad in 1867 was the catalyst for Amityville's second and more significant growth period. Prior to 1867 both commercial and residential development was centered around Merrick Road (South Turnpike then) between Park Avenue and the Amityville River. The intersection of Broadway and Merrick Road was the town's early epicenter boasting Ireland's Mill, the Ireland homestead, the First Methodist Church, the first school house, Dr. Richmond's home and office, the Post Office, various stores and the Amity Hotel, all within a two block walk.

With the location of the new train station a mile or so north of Merrick Road, at Broadway, the town center was inexorably pulled north as new development located close to that magnet. The logical first business to locate north was Wardle's Inn on Broadway adjacent to the railroad tracks, just a few steps from the station. In 1872 the first of many public school buildings for that location was erected at Park Avenue and Ireland Place. When the Triangle Building went up in 1892, the intersection of Broadway, Park Avenue and Ireland Place became the iconic center of town and remains so today.

In 1881 the Long Island Home for Nervous Invalids was built just north of the village and quickly became the town's largest employer. It was the first of four sanitariums and hospitals in Amityville and was followed closely by Louden Hall Sanitarium in 1886 and Brunswick Home and Hospital in 1888. These businesses attracted physicians and well

6.1 The Long Island Home for Nervous Invalids from a post card ca. 1910.

trained staffs to the area and catered to wealthy but "nervous" New Yorkers adding greatly to the local economic engine. The result was more and more demand for housing, goods and services which begat more new businesses creating yet more demand for housing, goods and services- a fortuitous economic engine. Amityville saw significant growth in population, infrastructure, commerce and housing during those late nineteenth century years.

It is not surprising that Ocean Avenue saw similar growth during this time as the town prospered and residents looked for areas to build homes with their new found wealth. An 1873 survey map of Amityville shows just a few Ocean Avenue dwellings at the north end at Merrick Road. Two Ireland homes sat on Merrick Road, one each on either side of Ocean Avenue, across the street from their mill and pond. There was another Ireland house shown just a little south on the river and a "Kartwright" residence, likely the same Bernard "Kortright" for whom Frank Wicks built a catboat in the late 1890s. But that was it for houses. We can assume a number of baymen moored their boats along the river and worked from there but lived elsewhere.

With similar timing to the village growth, Ocean Avenue had its beginning as a prime residential location. Frank Wicks began his ferry service to the ocean beaches from the Amityville River in 1875 so we can assume he started his Ocean Avenue business at that time and resided there as well. Dr. George Richmond built his home and office atop Richmond Avenue in 1845 but moved it to Ocean Avenue in 1876. Other notable Ocean Avenue residences were built before the turn of the century: Erastus Ketchum built a home for E.C. Smith in 1890, The Griffith's House (1894) was the first home built well south on Ocean Avenue(#278), and the Woodman House was completed in 1895.

Other Amityville River related commercial developments paralleled Ocean Avenue's residential growth. The Gilbert Rod and Gun Club was built on the east bank of the

6.2 The Gilbert Rod & Gun Club. Our house at 260 Ocean Avenue would be built right across from here on the west bank of the river in 1925 or so.

The Yacht Club and the End of the Beginning

river in 1884 as a hunting and fishing retreat for a group of wealthy Brooklynites and New Yorkers. Some time in the 1880s the Ocean Point Hotel was built on the water at the foot of Ocean Avenue and John Heinley started his coal business in 1890. John Ireland developed the New Point Hotel in 1892 with the Hathaway House following in 1900. Ocean Avenue and the Amityville River had become the go-to destination for discriminating vacationers and home builders.

With that bit of preamble we come to the Unqua Corinthian Yacht Club; what I like to think of as the end of the beginning of the Ocean Avenue story.

The Ireland meadows was a large part of the southern half of Ocean Avenue. Now the salt hay marshes were fast becoming the site for grand homes and hotels. In 1900 John Ireland and a group of Amityville sailors got together to form a yacht club. Ireland donated a piece of land at the end of Ocean Avenue which was the eastern most tip of the original West Neck, quintessentially early bay-centric Amityville. The yacht club begins their story this way:

> Unqua Corinthian Yacht Club, located in Amityville, New York on the Great South Bay, is a private membership club dedicated to activities including day boating, cruising, competitive sailing, recreational and competitive swimming, and fine dining and entertainment. On September 7, 1900, the yacht club was incorporated, and on November 12, 1900 received the blessing of the (New York) Supreme Court. John Ireland solved the first formidable problem of "where to build the club" by donating the original land. Then, spring 1901, the present clubhouse was constructed with a large central hall and porches on three sides. To reach the club from Ocean Avenue, trees were laid as a base for a wagon road over the mud and grass of the salt marsh. There was also a boardwalk for people on foot, and a pipeline for the club's water (which nearly boiled under the summer sun by the time it reached the club).

6.3 A photo of the Unqua Corinthian Yacht Club as it looked in the early 1900s.
Photo courtesy the Unqua Corinthian Yacht Club

The Yacht Club would become a fixture in Amityville culture and history and provide the dot on the exclamation point that is Ocean Avenue. For my time in Amityville, Ocean Avenue was not just where I lived but my axis of activity with the Yacht Club at the south and the high school at the north. For ten years my summer days were spent at the Yacht Club and evenings at the high school tennis courts. For two exceptional summers I was a sailing instructor at the Yacht Club.

During Ocean Avenue's golden years, 1900 to 1930, the southern tip of the street included the Palmer House, the most grand Victorian home on the avenue, the village dock with the terminus of the Cross-Island Trolley and ferry service to the ocean beaches, the Narragansett Inn, O'Brien's Beach, Lawrence B. Sperry's boathouse and guided missile testing site and the Unqua Corinthian Yacht Club.

To my eye the year 1900 marks a significant juncture in the development of Ocean Avenue as the prime residential street it is today. The street's 19th Century story line revolves around early commerce and the support of the bay trades- boat building, fishing, clamming, oystering and salt hay farming. The start of the Yacht Club and the turn of the century mark the emergence of Ocean Avenue as a recreational and residential mecca. The first quarter of the 20th Century would see most of the street built-out, especially the waterfront property. And as we have seen, the rising land value for residential use has almost completely pushed out the commercial entities.

It is this prime residential environment that attracted the folks that will complete my Golden Avenue story.

CHAPTER 7 - THE CROSS-ISLAND TROLLEY LINE

The 19th Century was certainly the age of rail in the United States and that mentality persisted well into the early part of the 20th Century. The long-line railroads had dominated the freight and passenger transportation picture with local networks of trolley lines filling the need for passenger service in the ever expanding large and small cities across the country.

Brooklyn is a good example of the use of trolleys for passenger travel. There were so many trolley lines criss-crossing Brooklyn, their favorite baseball team got the nickname the Brooklyn "Trolley Dodgers" because of the tracks that ran along the outfield borders.

In 1890 a trolley line was created running first from Halesite (the Huntington waterfront) to Huntington's Main Street then, soon after, to the Long Island Railroad Station in Huntington. Operated by the Huntington Railroad, it was a subsidiary of the Long Island Railroad and the main purpose was to offer passenger service to and from the railroad station.

At this time it was a "horse car" trolley system but the LIRR had public plans to electrify the line, which it did in 1898. Around the turn of the century the Railroad began formulating plans to expand the line south through Melville and Farmingdale to the LIRR station in Amityville then south to the Amityville village dock.[1]

---

1   Seyfried, Vincent F., *The Cross-Island Line, The Story of The Huntington Railroad*: (Garden City, L.I., 1976), 31.

THE CROSS-ISLAND TROLLEY LINE

The R. R. Station and Trolley, Trestle, Amityville, L. I.

7.1 A view of the Amityville train station, looking West, with the Cross-Island Trolley trestle with crossing trolley in the background.

The most obvious goal for this expansion was to create better access to the LIRR train station in Amityville. But there seemed to be an interest, at least in the eyes of the LIRR, in reuniting Huntington and Amityville from both a social and commercial standpoint. Certainly an admirable goal but one that would prove elusive. While the two towns, with such a familial past, lie only 20 miles apart, the opening of the railroad line through Amityville, from Brooklyn and New York, forever severed those family bonds. By 1900 Amityville was more closely aligned with Brooklyn by virtue of the summer renters, hotel visitors and the growing number of new residents fleeing the crowded metropolitan area. It is a curious fact that all the initial investors in the Huntington Railroad were residents of New York, New Jersey and Brooklyn.[2]

---

2   Ibid, 11.

The Golden Avenue

So starting about 1906 the Long Island Railroad began the process of getting town approvals and rights-of-way to extend the trolley line to Amityville. This followed an attempt in 1905 to build a line by a competing group of New York capitalists. The Amityville town fathers had decided to play hardball with this group and nothing ever came of it. Many locals now felt the trolley line was crucial for the town's success so the LIRR interest was welcomed. However, the Amityville town board continued to make the process difficult so in 1907[3] the LIRR announced they would bypass Amityville and proceeded with talks with the village of Babylon. The ploy worked. Amityville was forced to reexamine its position and some behind the scenes negotiation, led by Samuel Hildreth, a local attorney, produced an agreement in late 1907. The terms of the agreement were, in part, picky and arbitrary but the deal was important to the Railroad and they went forward.

It is interesting to note that the road from Huntington south to Amityville was considered too tortuous and unfit to accommodate the trolley tracks so a new route was proposed and approved by the state. The new road would be a straight, four lane macadam highway with the trolley tracks on its west side. The road would carry the New York State highway designation Route 110.

In 1905 the Long Island Automobile Observation Company began passenger car service between Huntington and Amityville, running one daily round-trip during the summer months, which was profitable. This automotive alternative to a dedicated, capital intensive rail system would ultimately be the downfall of the Huntington Railroad as well as almost every trolley system in America. Car and bus alternatives would challenge the Cross-Island Line every time there was any kind of service disruption but the owners, as well as local city planners, seemed rooted to a rail solution. As late as 1920 when the Huntington Railroad line was battling to stay alive, the notion that the automobile just

---

3   Ibid, 37.

7.2 The first day of operation through Amityville. The trolley is turning south on Broadway from Greene Avenue.

might provide a better solution to passenger travel was still years away.

So in May of 1909 the line was operating through Farmingdale and by August of that year the Cross-Island Trolley reached the Merrick Road in Amityville.

On August 23rd, 1909, the first run of the new line from Huntington to Amityville was made. And it was a very big deal, indeed. The opening ceremony was held at the Triangle Building in Amityville with State Assemblyman Alfred E. Smith the keynote speaker. Smith would go on to become Governor of New York (twice) and Democratic Presidential candidate in 1928. Vincent F. Seyfried in his book *The Cross-Island Line, The Story of the Huntington Railroad* describes the start of the first run following the elaborate ceremony and speeches. "At 11:AM the parade of ten trolley cars left for Farmingdale. First came a flat car with the military band, followed by a decorated float featuring the queen, miss Dorothy Sammis, enthroned under a white arch and escorted by her ladies in

7.3 The village was decked out for the ceremonies on the first day of service of the Cross-Island Trolley. The iconic Triangle building is just behind the trolley car.

waiting. Behind came the ten trolley cars with seats assigned to all those who had bought tickets for the dinner at the Beaux Arts Ball."[4]

Seyfried tells of that first ride and fuels the unkind characterization of Amityville folk as backward and withdrawn, "People from Amityville and vicinity who had never ventured more than a few miles beyond the village in their narrow, limited lives were lured from their homes for the first time by the trolley and were astounded at how big the world was. A "Brooklyn Times" reporter, who sat with four men from Amityville, pointed out to them different points of interest along the way, and when the old homestead in which Walt Whitman was born was reached, the reporter enthusiastically exclaimed: "Here's the famous old Walt Whitman homestead!" The visitors looked the little old weather-beaten

---

4   Ibid, 49.

house over in surprise, and then in one breath asked, "Who is he?"[5]

In May of 1910 the final leg to Amityville's town dock was completed. Part of the contention between the Amityville town board and the Huntington Railroad was the route through lower Amityville. The proposed route was down Broadway, across Merrick Road and down Bennett Place, East on Grace Place (now Grace Court) to Ocean Avenue, then south to the village dock at the foot of Ocean Avenue. This route was changed, we can assume, due to objections by the well-heeled Ocean Avenue residents who thought better of trolley tracks in their front yard. The new route took the trolley down Bennett Place then west through property owned previously by Mary P. Myton, Grace M. Ireland and Samuel P. Hildreth.[6] That new road was called Hildreth Court[7] running westward to Richmond Avenue. The trolley line then headed south on Richmond Avenue. At that time

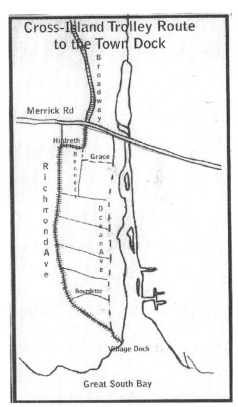

7.4 The route of the trolley line is shown down Richmond Ave. with the originally proposed route down Ocean Avenue shown as a dotted line.

5   Ibid, 59.

6   Ibid, 35.

7   That is the same Judge Hildreth that gave Moses the information about the legal status of the bay and island rights off Babylon and led the negotiation for the Cross-Island Line through Amityville.

Richmond Avenue did not run through to Ocean Avenue but stopped at Bourdette Place. This necessitated the connection of the foot of Richmond Avenue to the town dock, which was done.[8]

As of May 19, 1910 the complete line was operating. It was at this time the ferry captains, operating out of the Amityville River, included a stop at the town dock to pick up passengers delivered by the trolley. Company records indicate that special excursions were organized by the Cross-Island Line to connect with and support the Ocean Avenue island ferries.

One journalist wrote of his experience with this modern transportation miracle. He started out in Connecticut one fine summer day and travelled by packet boat to Huntington then caught the Cross-Island Trolley to the Amityville village dock where he boarded a ferry to Hemlock Beach. After spending a pleasant day at the ocean he made the reverse trip to Connecticut and marveled that he did it all in one day. We would be hard pressed to accomplish this today with any combination of public transit.

We can only guess at the activity level at the trolley terminus during the summer months in the years of 1910 to 1919. You had the village dock with working bay boats, small boats for hire, the ferry boats picking up and dropping off passengers, the Narraganset Hotel, O'Brien's Beach for swimming and the Unqua Corinthian Yacht Club just down at the end of Unqua Place. If there was a golden age and golden spot for Amityville, this was it.

But, alas, the existence of the Cross-Island Trolley was short lived. The southern portion, from Melville to Amityville, was never profitable. The trolley never did reconnect Amityville and Huntington, either socially or commercially, and we can guess that providing better access to the train station was not a benefit to the "narrow, limited" residents of Amityville who seldom ventured far from home. Obviously the ridership created by the activities around the village dock was not enough to compensate for the

---

8   The village allowed this with the provision that, should the trolley line cease operation, the right-of-way became the property of the village. This occurred in 1919.

general business malaise of the southern portion of the line.

Following the line's shutdown in 1919 the Huntington portion was operated in a court directed receivership by the Huntington Traction Co. while a buyer was sought. None was found and, in 1927, following eight years of limited success, the line was closed for good.[9] For good or bad, the age of the automobile had claimed yet another trolley line.

9   It is interesting to note that the performance of the Amityville section was bad enough that while the Huntington section was being operated in receivership, looking for a buyer, the tracks in Amityville were pulled up by a local scrap dealer in1920, netting $34,567.

CHAPTER 8- LAWRENCE SPERRY AND EARLY FLIGHT

On the southeast corner of Ocean Avenue and Unqua Place, where Richmond Avenue joins in, there is a marble monument with brass plaque which reads:

FIRST GUIDED MISSILE

September 11, 1916

Here Lawrence B. Sperry first demonstrated

to the US Navy personnel the Sperry Aerial

Torpedo - the first guided missile

Presented by Sperry Gyroscope Company during

1960, Centennial year of Dr. Elmer A. Sperry,

scientist and inventor

I must have walked past that monument 500 times on my way back and forth to the yacht club and never knew it was there. But I should have because Lawrence Sperry was a really big deal in the early days of aviation and, despite a short life (he died at the age of 31), he was such a force in the development of aeronautic safety many of his patents are still in effect today.

It took William Davenport, in his book *GYRO!: The Life and Times of Lawrence*

8.1 The Sperry plaque at the corner of Ocean Avenue and Unqua Place.

Sperry, to chronicle the exploits and inventions of this aviation pioneer. The book reads more like a Hollywood screen play with Errol Flynn cast as the intrepid aviator. The opening chapter tells of a particular event in Sperry's career that so captures his spirit and character it demands to be told first.

The setting was the Dayton Air Show of 1918. Considered the cradle of aviation at the time because of the early work of the Wright Brothers, Dayton's McKook Field was the site of an air show to strut the aeronautic stuff that was well on the way to defeating Kaiser Wilhelm in the First World War. And Lawrence Sperry was well on his way to becoming recognized as the most important force in the area of aviation safety, having already demonstrated the gyrostabilizer and the first, unmanned, guided missile. His goal for the air show was to personally demonstrate his new design for a pack parachute.

But Elmer Sperry, Lawrence's father, agreed with the Navy that Lawrence should not personally demonstrate the parachute and his seat on the Naval Consulting Board gave him that authority. He was at the air show with his good friend Thomas Alva Edison, who also sat on the Board. Young Lawrence held the rank of ensign in the Navy due to the top secret work he was doing for them with his aerial torpedo. To be sure Lawrence obeyed this order they had employees of the air field steal and hide the parachute. This was the first clue to their fiery father/son relationship.

During the air show Edison changed his seat to be with Lawrence and his pretty new bride, the silent screen actress, Winifred Allen. Edison, at 71 years old, still had an eye for the young ladies and Winifred had a special attraction; she had perfect diction and the stone deaf Edison had been reading her lips from the silver screen he had himself invented.[1] It didn't take Winifred long to beguile the star struck Edison and coax the location of the hidden parachute.

Ducking the Navy's flight ban, Sperry Junior hailed an Army aviator friend and his two-seater Lepere Liberty airplane, donned his flight gear and set off to collect the hidden parachute.

The parachute jump went beautifully and the crowd cheered as the chute opened. But the wind picked up and Lawrence's path was not back to the ground at the air field but directly toward downtown Dayton. As luck (or misfortune) would have it Lawrence's parachute caught on the roof of the tallest building in downtown Dayton, the Dayton Savings and Trust Building, also home to the U. S. Aeroplane Production Department and the Aircraft Experimental Depot. The fire department arrived, with its twelve-man round net, ready to catch the parachutist now dangling eleven stories above the street.

The fire department made its way to the roof to free the entangled parachute but Lawrence had other plans. He climbed up the shrouds of the parachute to a cornice above. Davenport describes the scene this way.

---

1   William Wyatt Davenport, *GYRO!; The Life and Times of Lawrence Sperry*, (Charles Scribner's Sons, New York, 1978), 6

LAWRENCE SPERRY AND EARLY FLIGHT

"He's made it. He's done it," they shouted, as Lawrence reached the
cornice and sat there with his legs dangling 150 feet above the street.

"All right just sit there," the fire chief bellowed through his megaphone.

Lawrence responded to this by standing on the cornice.

It was a purely decorative cornice, one foot wide. Its architect
had never conceived of it as a parachute hook.

Lawrence waived reassuringly to the crowd, which had fallen suddenly
silent. Then he went over and began to disentangle the shrouds and the
yards of Japanese silk that were caught on the angle of the cornice.

...Lawrence had gotten the chute pretty well disentangled. A
puff of the north wind had inflated a section of it. The shrouds
were free of the cornice. The helmeted firemen appeared on
the roof. They were lowering a ladder to the cornice.

Lawrence was having none of that. He flexed his knees. He sat
down again on the cornice, grasping the shrouds of his parachute.
He edged his leather bottom along the narrow shelf of stone until
he was straddling the corner. The silk streamed out, the air rushed
into the parachute, and he let it drag him off the cornice.

... The twelve firemen holding the net moved into position. They flexed
their knees, awaiting the impact of a hurtling body. But Lawrence
floated down, light as a thistle under the canopy of his parachute.
The firemen caught him in their net. He bounced up once, as though

in slow motion, then settled into the net under billows of silk.[2]

Indeed, "Icarus had disobeyed Daedalus, flown too high- and survived."[3] It is against this sub plot of the disapproving yet admiring father and daring but reckless son that we follow Lawrence Sperry's story to his flying boathouse at the foot of Ocean Avenue where much of his greatness would be demonstrated.

The Sperrys moved to Brooklyn in 1903, Lawrence's eleventh year. The Wright Brothers' first flight of that year would be the most galvanizing event in young Sperry's life. Flying became his passion and consumed his creative ambitions.

At 17, Lawrence enlisted the aid of his brother, Elmer Jr., and built a glider, copying one they had seen at an air show in nearby Mineola. To test it they towed it behind a car on a local race track. Lawrence's first untethered flight occurred when the tow rope broke; he was 150 feet in the air and brought the glider safely back to earth.

Thanks to a local patron the boys purchased a radial engine for the glider and Lawrence made his first powered flight that year in 1909, just six years after the Wright Brothers' first flight. On his first powered flight Lawrence took the plane to 500 feet and, more importantly, landed it safely. He was hooked.

Young Lawrence's passion did not fit well with a traditional education and he was prone to cutting school to work on his plane. He was not a good student and struggled with the structure and formality of learning. He would rather be making and doing.

Elmer Sperry, Sr. was a very successful inventor and marketer and had a path in mind for Lawrence. He envisioned an engineering degree from Cornell, Elmer's alma mater, then Lawrence would devote his energies to the family business, preferably behind a desk. To do this they first had to get Lawrence ready for Cornell so he was shipped off to a top-notch, mid-western boarding school for some much needed college preparatory

---

2   Ibid, 13-14
3   Ibid, 15

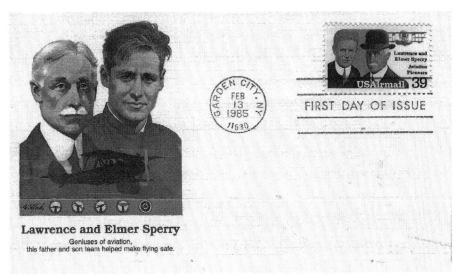

Lawrence and Elmer Sperry
Geniuses of aviation,
this father and son team helped make flying safe.

8.2 The first day of issue postcard featuring Elmer and Lawrence Sperry with their 1985 airmail stamp.

work (and well away from his airplane). Near graduation Lawrence sent his parents a letter laying out his reasons for wanting to pass on a college education in favor of full-immersion into the field of aviation. Finally convinced, his father packed off both Lawrence and his plane to Hammondsport, NY, to the Glenn Curtiss flying school.

It was with Curtiss that Lawrence was given the nickname "Gyro" for his pioneering work with the gyrocompass and on October 15, 1913 he received Federal Aeronautics Pilot License No. 11 from the Aero Club of America. At 21, Sperry became the youngest licensed pilot in America.

The concept of a gyroscopic based stabilizer for airplanes intrigued Lawrence and his work followed on a gyro stabilizer his father had invented and perfected for large ocean going vessels. To work for an airplane the device would need to control the three flight axes of yaw, pitch and roll and be small enough to fit on a plane.[4] After leaving the Curtiss

---

4   The Sperry Gyroscope for sea going vessels was the size of a room.

school, Lawrence joined his father's company, Sperry Gyroscope, to develop this new device for the nascent airplane industry.

Working for dad wasn't so easy. Lawrence wanted to be in the air and dad wanted him behind a desk. And Lawrence found the company to be rigid and not open to new ideas and directions. Worst of all, Lawrence was given the newly created Aeronautic Division to develop but the company management, including his father, believed airplanes were still a dangerous hobby with little growth potential. And this, after Lawrence had won first prize at the International Airplane Safety Competition in France in 1914. He and his co-pilot made the final pass of their demonstration each standing on a wing with the auto pilot flying the plane. But, lacking a shared vision and battling his father at every turn, Lawrence would leave Sperry Gyroscope and set out to create his own company.

Young Sperry's early development work with the Navy started in 1916 while he was still working for his father. This was the secret aerial torpedo project and Sperry chose to build his hanger and shop at the foot of Ocean Avenue adjacent to the Narragansett Hotel. The location was sufficiently out of the way to avoid prying eyes (at least in the non-summer months) yet accessible by train and trolley, and the hotel gave him a convenient place to stay during extended trials. The work shop and boat house provided storage for his amphibious biplane and the Great South Bay was a reasonably safe and uninhabited area for the many series of test flights that were planned.

The Amityville location would be much in the news as Lawrence and his pioneering exploits were reported in the press. In September, 1916, *Air Age Weekly* ran a full page article about the inauguration luncheon of the New York Flying Yacht Club. They reported that six of the attendees had arrived by airplane which they surmised was the first time this had ever happened. "Lawrence B. Sperry, with Ralph Bowman, was the second to arrive. He left Amityville, L.I., at 12:02 and, circling over Coney Island and Fort Hamilton, came to the Battery and up the river, making the landing shortly before 1 o'clock. As he volplaned to the water both he and Bowman threw their hands up and let the boat make its own landing. The Sperry stabilizer brought it down as softly as the alighting of a feather."[5]

Also in that same issue of *Aerial Age Weekly* was an article titled "Lawrence B. Sperry Makes Night Flying Demonstration." The day after the N.Y. Flying Club luncheon Sperry flew from Moriches to Amityville, at night, using his auto pilot system and lights under the wings to light the way. This was a monumental achievement for 1916 when typical flying was done only during the day when the pilot could be within eyesight of his route.[6]

With the opening of hostilities in France in 1917, Sperry volunteered to serve in the Air Corps in the First World War but was refused because he lacked a college education. Through his development work with the Navy he was eventually given the rank of ensign[7] but saw no action in the war. The Navy deemed his importance in aircraft development and safety more important than his possible contributions in harms way.

It was during this time that Lawrence gave flying lessons in his spare time. His students tended to be young, attractive females. One November day he was giving a lesson to a young, married woman and their plane crashed in the bay somewhere off Babylon. Two duck hunters saw the crash and rushed to give assistance. They found the two aviators naked and alive, but banged up a bit. Lawrence spent a few days in the hospital with more damage to his pride than his hide.

Sperry would later attribute the lack of clothing to the force upon impact with the water, but that wasn't repeated too often. The press was kept out of the affair so it did not get any publicity. The good news seemed to be that the crash had nothing to do with a failure of the auto pilot but everything to do with someone accidentally turning it off during the more active part of the "training" flight. So one more first was attributed to

---

5   Aerial Age Weekly, INAUGURATION LUNCHEON N. Y. FLYING YACHT CLUB, September 11, 1916

6   It is interesting to note that the first maps for pilots were strip maps assembled from automotive maps with notations of significant landmarks observable from above.

7   It was this commission that gave the Navy the authority to forbid him from demonstrating his new parachute design at the Dayton Air Show in 1918. This after some near catastrophes during testing of the arial torpedo which had the Navy questioning his judgement.

AERIAL AGE WEEKLY, September 11, 1916

Lawrence B. Sperry Makes Night Flying Demonstration

The first demonstration of the possibility of water flying at night was given under the auspices of the Aero Club of America, September 1, by Lawrence B. Sperry, the youthful inventor, who flew from Moriches to Amityville, fifty miles away, in pitch dark, lighting his way over the dark waters of the bay with specially arranged lights attached to his aeroplane, and guiding his course by compass.

Mr. Sperry, accompanied by his mechanic, started from Moriches at 8:22 to fly to his hangar at Amityville. His flying boat was equipped with a new night flying outfit, constructed by Mr. Sperry, consisting of three searchlights, each of 53 candle-power attached to his lower wing, two of which were driven by a generator operated by a little windmill connected with the aeroplane. The other derived its power from a storage battery. In this way, if the two operated by the generator should fail, the one operated by the battery would be available, and vice versa. There were also attached to the wing tips of the aeroplane a green light on the starboard and a red light on the port side. After the lights were switched on and the aeroplane started, the machine sped through the black sky with weird effect. The machine, entirely operated by the Sperry automatic pilot, which controls its course and maintains its even keel, covered the distance between Moriches and Amityville in an hour and forty-five minutes, arriving at Amityville at 10:06.

The Aero Club officials consider the demonstration of far reaching importance. Mr. Henry Woodhouse, member of the Board of Governors of the Club, said that this demonstration was so successful that it proves that flying at night can be made as easy as flying during the day. This is another achievement to Mr. Sperry's long list of valuable inventions and accomplishments.

8.3 Sperry's night flying demonstration.

8.4 Lawrence B. Sperry

Lawrence B. Sperry- founding member of the Mile High Club.

In May of 1917 Sperry established his business, the Sperry Aircraft Company, in Farmingdale, L.I., just a few miles north of Amityville. The site provided the structures necessary for aircraft production and enough space for a runway capable of handling land based aircraft. It was here that Sperry produced his Messenger bi-plane and two land and sea amphibious planes for the Navy to use for coastal patrols. The air/sea capability would greatly improve their flexibility. This site would grow over the years to become the manufacturing location of the Fairchild Airplane Manufacturing Company then Republic Aviation starting in the World War II years and finally Zahn's airport which was, at one point, the largest private airport in the country.

It is also interesting to note that Sperry rented a house in Massapequa, NY, the next town west of Amityville, and shared the house with Grover Loening, another aviation pioneer. Loening would go on to start his own airplane manufacturing company in New York. It appears that these two bachelors cut a wide swath in the Long Island social scene.

In February of 1918 Sperry married the Hollywood starlet Winifred Allen and added to his growing list of firsts by flying from Amityville to Governor's Island with Miss Allen to be married. *Flying Magazine* called them "...the first couple to use an airplane to take an aerial honeymoon."

Ensign Lawrence B. Sperry, the noted inventor and expert aviator, made an addition to his already long list of achievements and distinctions. On February 19th he flew from Amityville to Governor's Island, New York, with Miss Winifred Allen, of New York, and got married. Then they flew back home — the first couple to use an aeroplane to take an aerial honeymoon

8.5 The Sperry's aerial honeymoon.

March 1918 saw the first unmanned, automatically controlled aerial torpedo which flew from the Amityville shore 1,000 feet out into the bay.

Following the end of WWI the Navy lost interest in the aerial torpedo and pulled their funding but the Army had interest and contracted Sperry in 1920 to experiment with his Messenger bi-plane as a remote controlled torpedo. This publicity photo from 1922 shows Sperry in the cockpit of his Messenger on Capitol Hill. It seems the Government checks were running slow so he flew to Washington and landed on the Capitol steps to raise awareness to his plight. He flew home with a check.

Sadly, it was in his trusty Messenger that Sperry went down in the English Channel on a cold December day in 1923, flying from England to France, hawking his auto pilot system. The plane was

8.6 The aerial torpedo is tested for aerodynamics on a car in Amityville.

Lawrence Sperry, piloting the Sperry plane which he claims is destined to become the "Fliver" of the air. Capable of making 100 miles an hour it can land in an ordinary roadway and park in a remarkably small space. Lincoln Memorial in background. 3/21/22

8.7 Sperry at the Capitol.

found intact about a mile from shore with Sperry's flight jacket aboard. It is surmised his engine failed and he could not make it back to shore. He apparently tried to swim to shore and succumbed to the frigid English Channel.

We can only guess what role Sperry might have played in the aeronautic industry had he not suffered that untimely death. However, those that knew him well and knew of the many close calls he had had, suggested it was just in his DNA.

Chapter 9- The Prohibition Years

Although the days of Prohibition seem like ancient history today, we moved back to Amityville in 1953 just 20 years after Prohibition's repeal. I grew up with stories about the rum running days while most of those involved were still around. I particularly remember my father talking about his father, Grandpa Robbie, walking from their Robbins Avenue home to the Ocean Avenue boatyard every Saturday, with milk pail in hand, to pick up his weekly supply of gin. That would have been in 1928 when they first moved to Amityville.

I distinctly remember going with Dad to Jim's Ocean Avenue Boatyard and playing on a rotting skeleton of a boat that was a barge used to move illicit booze from Jones Island to the Amityville River. We grew up with many legends about the local bootlegging activities. The stories conjured up visions of daring and exciting exploits on the bay but were always devoid of personal references. The tale might recount a near apprehension by a Coast Guard cutter but fail to mention who was piloting the boat. Or a boat would be described that had been specially outfitted to outrun the patrol boats but the owner of the boat would never be connected to the activities. There seemed to be an unwritten rule that, despite our admiration, our friends and neighbors should be protected from idle gossip about their illegal activities, regardless of how noble those activities appear today.

Everrett S. Allen, in his book *The Black Ships* puts the local rum runners' activities in perspective, "…these down-East sailors had a heritage of hardship and hard work, of simple lives and sacrifice, of persistent separation from family, because this is the way of seagoing. They were largely men more silent than talkative, fiercely industrious, exceptionally unafraid, generally unlettered, unassuming, more often than not. They became smugglers not because they were essentially devious or because they possessed any other qualifications for lawbreaking but because they were in the right place at the right time, possessed of the right skills, and they were short of cash."[1]

Prohibition in America was not just an early 20th Century phenomenon. The first indication we had a problem with alcohol was in pre-Revolutionary War Georgia. Public intoxication became so common the British instituted a prohibition of alcohol shipments to the colony. This didn't last. The local moonshiners simply stepped up production and the British merchants negatively affected by the ban petitioned Parliament and it was lifted. Commerce triumphed over sobriety but the problem wasn't solved.

The first challenge to our new nation and George Washington's presidency was the Whiskey Rebellion of 1794. The farmers of western Pennsylvania, lacking good transportation to ship their crops, chose to turn their harvested grain into alcohol and ship the more easily transported product to market. They also chose not to pay the Federal excise tax on these distilled spirits. In the country's infancy this was the only domestic tax levied by the Federal Government, all other Federal revenues came from import duties on foreign goods. President Washington was forced to raise a militia and he rode at its head to suppress the rebellion. No lives were lost but the excise tax on distilled spirits remained odious and a difficult tax to collect.

During the early 1800s the abuse of spirit beverages continued to grow, giving rise to organizations such as the Women's Christian Temperance Union (WCTU). Backed mainly by Protestant church organizations, their emphasis was on temperance. These activities had little impact and we watched the consumption of spirits rise leading to a broadening of the movement with the new goal of total prohibition. John Kobler, in his book *Ardent*

---

1   Allen, Everett S., *The Black Ships, Rumrunners of Prohibition*, (Commonwealth Editions, Carlisle, MA, 1979), 75

Spirits comments, "Like the first prohibition wave, the second [the late 1800's] was not accompanied by a decrease in the consumption of alcohol. On the contrary, it rose from an annual average of about 62,000,000 gallons of distilled liquor during the decade 1870-80 to more than 76,000,000 during the succeeding decade, from almost 21,000,000 gallons of wine to 27,500,000, and from 647,000,000 gallons of malt liquor to about 1 billion, all together representing an increase in the per capita consumption from 8.79 gallons to 13.21. These figures, computed by the U.S. Statistical Abstracts, could not, of course, include the incomputable amounts of illegal liquor consumed. ...bootleggers and speakeasies thrived wherever prohibitory laws existed."[2]

As the problem worsened the prohibition movement gained new champions with disparate incentives: the traditional base of women's organizations was joined by the established Protestant churches and industry leaders quietly joined as alcoholism on the job was bad for business. And the Southern states, without a significant position in distilled spirits production, realized prohibition would benefit their moonshining constituents. As our nation approached the hostilities of WWI there was a growing concern over the predominantly German controlled brewery industry.[3] Kobler notes, "...many of the country's most persuasive dry leaders...came chiefly from rural areas, bringing with them a curious traditional amalgam of liberalism and bigotry...they tended to equate rectitude, sobriety and piety with country life and vice, drunkenness and irreligion with the cities. The entire temperance movement came to reflect a conflict of cultures- agrarian against industrial, the native-born Yankee against the immigrant micks, dagos, bohunks and krauts, Protestants against Catholics and Jews, and by exploiting the prejudices of the rural masses the dry fanatics won their biggest following."[4]

2　　Kobler, John, *Ardent Spirits, The Rise and Fall of Prohibition*, (Putnam, New York, 1973), 160

3　　As late as the start of WWI the brewing industry still conducted its national meeting in German.

4　　Kobler, 168

THE PROHIBITION YEARS

Thus, with this unholy alliance and the national prejudices from World War I, the dry forces reached the tipping point in public sentiment and the Volstead Act was passed in January of 1919. Woodrow Wilson vetoed the bill on technical grounds but the veto was overridden by the Congress. Enactment would require ratification by 2/3 of the states but with 27 states already dry, the endorsement by Southern states and the popularity of the prohibition cause, this would prove to be an easy task. Ratification took less than a year and as of January 16, 1920 the United States was officially dry. Officially.

Although the majority of Americans were not in favor of Prohibition and most citizens first, didn't think the law would pass and, second, didn't think the 18th amendment would be ratified, organized crime was hard at work through the process to prepare for the worst. Although noble in spirit the Volstead Act was naive in thinking that a constitutional amendment could change the drinking habits of a nation. Edward Behr, in his book *Prohibition*, comments, "In retrospect, the Volstead Act was hopelessly inadequate, because it grossly underestimated the willingness of the lawbreakers to risk conviction, the degree of human ingenuity displayed to get around its provisions, and the ease with which the lawbreakers would be able to subvert all those whose job it was to enforce it."[5]

The naivety was confirmed when Congress allocated just $2.2 Million dollars to enforce the law and hired a force of just 1,500 Federal agents to do it. The already overburdened Coast Guard was entrusted with the daunting task of patrolling the Nation's coastline and Great Lakes to enforce a law that was poorly conceived and generally ignored by the average citizen with no increase in either ships or men. They didn't even get a piece of the paltry $2.2 million.

It is interesting, though, that organized crime spent their time leading up to the start of Prohibition by developing alternate sources for the soon to be illegal beer, wine

---

5   Behr, Edward, Prohibition, *Thirteen Years That Changed America*, (Arcade Publishing, New York, 1996), 79

and liquor that did not include delivery by sea. Early activity revolved around specially outfitted cars and trucks bringing booze in from Canada to the larger metropolitan areas along the northern part of the country. Another significant early source of illegal liquor was the production of spirits for "medicinal" purposes which was then re-labeled and shipped to the growing number of speakeasies in the country. In fact, thanks to a generally corrupt licensing system the production of medicinal whiskey products increased ten fold during prohibition.

9.1 McCoy's Arethusa. The Maritime Museum

Then in 1921 Bill McCoy got in the smuggling business and single-handedly created the Prohibition institution we know as "Rum Row." It started not so innocently with McCoy buying the 90 foot schooner *Henry L. Marshall* and sailing her to Nassau where he loaded up with 1500 cases of Canadian whiskey. He sailed to the Georgia coast, 20 miles south of Savannah, and delivered the haul to some local crime folks for $15,000.

He paid off the *Marshall* and bought the 130 foot *Arethusa*, his new flagship. This he loaded with 5,000 cases of brand name whiskey and sailed to New Jersey, delivering 2,000 cases to a client there. But McCoy was a smart businessman and realized that if he anchored in international waters and had his customers come to him, he was breaking no laws. All the risk was with the customers. So he sailed just off the coast of Long Island and got the word out that he was open for business and sold off the balance of the 3,000 cases in no time, mostly to locals in small boats.

Rum Row was born. Over the next few years hundreds of imitators would load up a variety of vessels and anchor off the coast, from Massachusetts to New Jersey, and sell their wares to all comers. McCoy further refined the process by moving his operation to the island of St. Pierre, a French colony and fishing village just off the coast of Newfoundland. The liquor was delivered to St. Pierre from European ports and transferred to the growing number of vessels that would sail south to Rum Row. A year after McCoy began using St. Pierre over 1,000 vessels would be recorded as having come and gone from this tiny island.[6] An officer from a Nova Scotia schooner was quoted as saying, "At night on Rum Row, you would think it was a city out there, off Jones Inlet, near the ship lane, or maybe twelve miles off Highland Light. It was like going to a supermarket."[7]

McCoy is also credited with the invention of the "ham" or "burlock," a burlap sack that was lighter than a case of liquor and more easily moved and stowed aboard the delivering ships. Six bottles were arranged in a pyramid, three bottles, then two, then one, and stitched in burlap with straw to cushion the fragile cargo. It is said that some rum runners would include blocks of salt in the hams in case the cargo had to be jettisoned to avoid capture by the Coast Guard. The salt packed hams would sink to the bottom but float to the surface after a few days as the salt dissolved, allowing the precious cargo to be reclaimed.

McCoy was not very lucky, though. In August of 1921 the *Marshall*, sailed by a second crew, was seized off the coast of New Jersey with 1,400 cases of whiskey aboard. The ship was well outside the 3 mile limit but the Feds invoked a provision of the Maritime Act of

---

6   Smuggling with the "Real McCoy," www.drinkingcup.net, accessed 12/19/2016

7   Allen, 43

9.2 Hams or burlocks being stowed in the forward hold.
The Maritime Museum

1790, assuming a 12 mile limit for vessels engaged in fraudulent pursuits. The courts went along.

McCoy continued rumrunning with the *Arethusa*, renamed *Tamoka* and sailing under British and French registry. In November of 1923 he was seized off the Coast of New Jersey. He spent two years on bail in New Jersey then plead guilty to all charges. He spent just nine months in jail and despite heavy defense costs he was able to retire from his life of crime and live comfortably until his death in 1948, at the age of 71.

The Rum Row McCoy created became a significant source of illegal booze. Some historians believe that as much as one third of all illegal liquor came in through that channel. It was a very sophisticated supply chain that began with European syndicates behind large shipments of liquor to St. Pierre, repackaging and transfer to smaller rum runners for delivery to Rum Row. Here the final step went to the local delivery boats that took the liquor from the supply boats and had to negotiate the waiting Coast Guard cutters and patrol boats. Again from *The Black Ships*, "The [custom marine] patrol guarded the coastlines of Connecticut, New York, Long Island, and New Jersey. "[Quoting Captain Peter J. Sullivan, the officer in charge of the custom marine patrol]...when it was initiated, liquor was entering Jones Inlet 'in a steady stream' and that Montauk, 'which was as bad as Atlantic Highlands, conditions were so easy that bootleggers would land, drive the natives off the beach, and then land their contraband in peace. It was a cinch for them.'"[8]

Harold Waters, in *Smugglers of Spirits* describes how the battle lines were formed, "The 'sunset fleet' of contact boats began to arrive toward evening... Their skippers shook their fists at our destroyers, as well as the six-bitter flotillas which had meanwhile taken station halfway between Rum Row and the Long Island shoreline. Still closer in, mounting guard over the approaches to the other landing places, were picket boats. Along the shoreline itself, patrolling the beaches were squads of armed sand pounders [Coast Guardsmen stationed on the shoreline]."[9] Described this way you would think there was no way to get past the ever ready Coast Guard but there is general agreement that the Coast Guard only stopped about 10% of illegal shipments through Rum Row.

The mention of the "sand pounders" is interesting. It appears that this shore duty was very unpopular with the Coast Guard officers and enlisted men so an outside crew was hired to perform this duty. I spoke with a North Carolinian who's father was recruited for this shore patrol in the 1920s but it is not clear when these patrols were active and how effective they were. It is common knowledge that the abandoned Life Saving Station at

---

8   Allen, 153

9   Waters, Harold, *Smugglers of Spirits, Prohibition and the Coast Guard Patrol*, (Hastings House, Publishers, New York, 1971), 68.

Gilgo Beach[10] was used by the Amityville rum runners to store liquor before transfer to bay boats for delivery to the mainland.

We need to remember that Robert Moses didn't complete the Ocean Causeway connecting Jones Beach to Fire Island until 1933 so during the Prohibition years there was no automotive access to the ocean beaches. This required any liquor landed on Jones Island be transported, again, by boat, across the bay, to safe points along the south shore of Long Island. Both Jones Inlet and Fire Island Inlet were heavily patrolled by the Coast Guard so entry there was difficult at best.

Local oral history has it that the Ocean Avenue baymen would collect a bunch of teenage boys and head off in the evening to the coves on the bay side of Jones Island around Gilgo or West Gilgo. From the ocean beach they would signal the delivery boats heading from the mother boats anchored on Rum Row. The delivery boats would get close enough to shore so their cargo could be dumped in the surf. Allen adds this to the story line. "The rumrunner, though known, was pursuable and arrestable only within very strictly defined limits- and he made the duration of these circumstances [possession] as brief as possible."[11] Here the teenage boys would gather up the booze and bring it to shore. It was then moved from the ocean beach to the waiting boats on the bay side. The bay boats would navigate through the islands and marshes that stand between Jones Island and the open bay. It was here that the shallow draft boats and skills of the baymen paid their dividends.

The Coast Guard also patrolled the bay so our intrepid baymen were still not home free. The bay boats used for transporting the goods were slow, more so fully laden with booze, and they had to make it across two miles of open water before reaching the relative safety of the boat yard.

---

10   The Life Saving Service was combined with the Coast Guard in 1915 and almost all of the Life Saving Stations were closed in favor of sea patrols.

11   Allen, 160

THE PROHIBITION YEARS

In 1925 the Coast Guard was given a sizable fleet of moth-balled navy ships from World War I including 20 destroyers and 300 various large and small vessels along with an additional 5,000 officers and men.[12] This more than doubled their manpower and allowed for a more aggressive strategy on Rum Row. With the beefed-up destroyer capability, the Coast Guard focused its efforts against the growing activity at sea and took a more passive approach to dealing with the locals on the bay. There had been a number of highly publicized encounters where Coast Guard cutters had fired on local boats resulting in loss of local lives. The papers had crucified the offending sailors and it is likely the Coast Guard brass decided to take the battle to the mother boats that could more easily be identified as "bad guys."

In an interesting side note, the ranks of the Coast Guard enlisted corps was 70% foreign with many not even English speaking, much less U.S. citizens. Waters, a Coast Guardsman and New Zealander himself, describes the attitude of the enlisted men: "The whys and wherefores of National Prohibition meant absolutely nothing to those of us who populated the enlisted ranks of the Coast Guard in the early Twenties. None of us regarded ourselves as crusaders dedicated to the total destruction of Demon Rum. Most of us were, on the other hand, on remarkably good terms with the Demon, having frolicked with him the Seven Seas over. Rather, we were to regard rum-chasing in the light of sport, as a glorified sort of cops and robbers game."[13]

* *

Our house at 260 Ocean Avenue was built in the mid-20s and it sat right on the water. The sun porch actually was built over an old boat slip. My friends always speculated there

---

12   Allen, 110.

13   Waters, 17.

9.3 Our house at 260 Ocean Avenue as seen from the Amityville River, ca 1958. The sun porch built over an old boat slip is to the left.

was a trap door in the floor of the sun porch so the booze from a boat, hidden in the old boat slip, could be passed up into the house. The old boat slip existed but completely protected by a solid bulkhead, which could have been a modern addition. But I can say with certainty that no trap door existed as of 1953 when we moved into the house. Not to say that the original owner hadn't removed the trap door after 1933 when it was no longer needed.

Once ashore, and the cargo stowed, all peril was gone. Prohibition was a Federal law and the meager funding for enforcement went to the Federal agencies so tasked- the FBI, Treasury, Justice Department, Prohibition Bureau and the Federal courts. In fact, the Democratic (wet) controlled New York State Congress, tired of being asked to enforce a law it didn't agree with and with no funding, repealed their Prohibition laws in 1923, leaving the entire burden of enforcement to the Federal Government. Towns like Amityville with strong ties to the bay community and a long history with the hospitality industry did more than just look the other way. Local lore has it that the police paddy wagon was used to deliver booze from the Ocean Avenue boat yard to thirsty citizens around town.

Prohibition ended up having the opposite effect on drinking in America than it set out to do. "In New York, whereas many great restaurants simply closed down, speakeasies proliferated on a truly startling scale. By 1922, there would be at least 5,000, and by 1927, over 30,000- twice as many as all legal bars, restaurants, and night clubs *before* Prohibition."[14] Kobler adds, "The New York *Telegram* once assigned a team of reporters to investigate the availability of liquor in the borough of Manhattan alone. They managed to buy it in 'dancing academies, drugstores, delicatessens, cigar stores, confectionaries, soda fountains, behind partitions of shoeshine parlors, back rooms of barbershops, from hotel bellhops, from hotel headwaiters, from hotel day clerks, in express offices, in motorcycle delivery agencies, paint stores, malt shops, cider stubes, fruit stands, vegetable markets, groceries, smoke shops, athletic clubs, grill rooms, taverns, chophouses, importing firms, tearooms, moving-van companies, spaghetti houses, boarding-houses, Republican clubs, Democratic clubs, laundries, social clubs, newspapermen's associations.'"[15]

Behr points to Prohibition as the catalyst for a change in America's drinking habits. "There was an almost immediate, nationwide change in drinking habits. It became the thing to do, among students, flappers, and respectable middle-class Americans all over the country, to defy the law- as much a manifestation of personal liberty as a thirst for

---

14   Behr, 87

15   Kobler, 234-5

alcohol."[16] What was once a male, all-day, often solitary addiction became a celebration of both sexes and a very social activity. Women began to bear their share of our national problem with alcohol.

"Congress initially appropriated a mere $2,200,000. In 1921 the appropriation was three times that much. In 1926 it came to almost $10,000,000, and so it went until 1929 when new Prohibition Commissioner, James M. Doran, informed Congress that any serious attempt to enforce the law would cost at least $300,000,000. Congress gave him $12,000,000."[17]

In 1933 Prohibition ended, first with a return to "real beer" in the Spring, then with the repeal of the 18th amendment, the only constitutional amendment ever to be repealed. Many consider the enactment of the 18th amendment and the subsequent 13 years under Prohibition to be the low point in American self-governance.

The story of the Ocean Avenue rum runners is but one of thousands along Long Island's south shore; a different story for every creek, bay, inlet or cove that offered shelter for the veritable army of bay boats that answered the thirst of our nation. Not a proud time for the Great South baymen but a testament to their industry and creativity. At a time when the country was heading toward the Great Depression the best explanation for this illegal activity was it paid better than clamming and fishing.

---

16   Behr, 89.

17   Kobler, 338

CHAPTER 10- LITTLE MISS SURE SHOT

Much of the early Ocean Avenue development was in summer housing for the well-heeled New York City crowd. The *Amityville Record*, from the teens and twenties, is full of the Spring comings and Fall goings of the social set. Combined with the local resort hotels Amityville was host to an impressive list of the who's who from those days. One improbable Ocean Avenue renter was Annie Oakley, arguably the most famous sharp shooter in American History.

Born Phoebe Ann Mosey[1] in Darke County Ohio, 1860, Annie had a difficult childhood. The family were subsistence farmers and she lost her father to pneumonia when she was six years old. Unable to support the children, her mother was forced to send Annie, age 10, and a younger sister, to the Darke County Infirmary or local "poor farm." From there she was placed with an area family to help the wife and new baby with the promise of 50 cents a week and an education. Neither materialized. The family was really looking for an older boy to help with the farm chores and little Annie was put to the task. She was denied the promised schooling and was physically and mentally abused by the couple. Letters to and from her mother were never delivered.

At twelve years old Annie ran away and, with the help of strangers, was able to find

---

1   There is much debate over the spelling of the last name. Oakley contended that the name was "Mosey" which is engraved on her father's tombstone. This is the spelling endorsed by the Annie Oakley Foundation. In various places we see "Mauzy," "Moses" and "Mosie." In 1884 two of Annie's brothers and one sister changed their names to Moses.

her way home. She went back to the poor farm and flourished under the kindly care and attention of the couple who ran the farm. Annie learned to sew and helped with the administrative function of the farm, skills which served her well in later years.

At age 15 Annie was able to rejoin her family. It was at this time that Annie began hunting to help feed the family and demonstrated the shooting skills that would make her famous. She became a market hunter supplying all manner of birds and game that found its way to Cincinnati hotels and restaurants. The proceeds from hunting enabled her to pay off the mortgage on her mother's farm.

The Annie Oakley legend began in 1881[2] when Frank Butler came to the area. Butler had a traveling sharp shooting act and was performing in North Star, Ohio. He always threw out a $100 challenge to any local shooter who could best him in a match. He was surprised to see the pretty, petite, and demure young Annie as his opponent and even more surprised when he missed his 25th bird and lost the match.

Annie joined Butler and they were married in 1882. Butler's partner in the shooting act, John Graham, became ill and Annie was pressed into service as Frank's assistant, throwing targets, reloading guns, etc. But it quickly became apparent that Annie was the better shot and their roles were reversed with Frank then supporting Annie's shooting. Annie took the stage name Oakley, and the most famous shooting act of all times was born. Uncharacteristic for the time, Frank was happy to become the support for Annie and spent the rest of his life successfully managing her career.

In 1884 Annie and Frank joined the Sells Circus, traveling to 187 cities in 13 states throughout the Mid-west. It was here Annie met and befriended Sitting Bull who gave her the name Watanya Cecelia or Little Sure Shot. Future press literature claimed Sitting Bull

---

2   That made Annie 21 years old but the legend says she was just 15. It seems that later in her career Annie had a 15 year old female marksman competitor in the Buffalo Bill Wild West Show and, in an act of sleight-of-age, Annie's true 26 years were magically changed to 20. This 6 year discrepancy would pop up every time anyone tried to work backwards in Annie's career.

10.1 An Annie Oakley shooting exhibition. Husband Frank Butler is crouched behind the gun table.

adopted Annie as she reminded him of his daughter lost in a cavalry raid years before. The adoption was never recorded and it is doubtful it ever happened.

The Sells Circus finished in December of 1884 in New Orleans where Annie and Frank first met Buffalo Bill Cody. Their first meeting did not result in an offer to join Cody's Wild West Show but a second chance came in April of 1885 in Louisville, KY, when Annie joined the show, billed as "Annie Oakley, the peerless wing and rifle shot."[3] She would spend a total of 16 years with Buffalo Bill's Wild West Show, and almost from the start commanded the highest salary of all the acts, except Buffalo Bill himself. According to *Billboard* in 1911, Annie Oakley was "the best paid arena star for a quarter of a century."[4]

---

3   Kasper, Shirl, *Annie Oakley*: (University of Oklahoma Press, 1992), 41.

4   Ibid, 191.

THE GOLDEN AVENUE

By 1902 Annie and Frank had retired from the Wild West Show and settled into a routine of summers in New York or New England and winters in Florida or North Carolina. The Wild West Show had made them nomads and they never had known a place of their own. They did try home ownership and built a house in Nutley, New Jersey but sold it in 1904, preferring hotel living instead.[5]

It was in 1904 that Annie's connection with Amityville and Ocean Avenue began, and it started with a performance of the hit musical comedy *The Wizard of Oz* in New York City. Annie and Frank had attended a performance and were so taken with the show and Fred Stone's scarecrow character they went backstage to meet the actor. This first meeting led to a dinner where the Butlers and Stones discovered a shared love of things Western, especially shooting. They also shared the traditional values of thrift, decency, morality, and sobriety, all in short supply in the early 20th Century entertainment business. Both Oakley and Stone would have solid, lifelong marriages, not at all common among entertainers and actors.

Fred Stone began his show business career at eleven as a high wire performer in the circus. Teamed with his younger brother, and with support from their parents, they traveled with small "wagon" circuses perfecting their acrobatics and multi-task circus talents including playing in the band, black-face song and dance, clowning, high-wire artistry and any other bit parts required of all members of a very small circus troupe.

Fred's physical comedic talents and song and dance background combined with his co-star Dave Montgomery's yin to his yang, got them the leads in *The Wizard of Oz* which opened in New York in 1902. Montgomery and Stone were a smash hit, playing in *Oz* for an unprecedented four years. Together they would star in hit after hit musical comedies including *The Red Mill* (1906), *The Old Town* (1910), *The Lady of the Slipper* (1912), *Chin*

---

5   Kasper tells the humorous story about the design of the Nutley house. Annie had all the bedrooms built without closets, apparently preferring to live out of a steamer trunk as they had done for so many years on the road.

Chin (1914), and *Jack O'Lantern* (1917). Following Dave Montgomery's death in 1917 Fred continued alone but began bringing his daughters into his shows with him. All three daughters ended up with significant stage careers. Stone would complete his career first in silent films then talkies.

About the time Oakley and Stone first met he bought a house and two acre plot on the west bank of the Naraskatuck River in Amityville. He was firmly in the New York theater mode then and it was safe to settle into a place that allowed him easy access to New York and the theater but enough space to do the things he loved to do- ride horses with his family and sail. Later he would acquire additional land and add a polo field where his Sunday matches often included Will Rogers, Vernon Castle (of the dancing Castles) and Douglas Fairbanks.[6]

Stone also had a very close relationship with Will Rogers and his family. Rogers spent so much time at the Stone's house he ended up buying the property across the street and became their neighbor in Amityville. Rogers' three children were the same ages as the three Stone daughters and they spent much time together, often on horseback.[7]

Stone spoke very warmly about his friendship with Annie Oakley. Early in his Amityville years the Butlers spent the entire summer with them. This would likely have been around 1907. He mentions a clay pigeon tournament at the house in that year with Annie putting on a demonstration for the contestants.[8] The Buffalo Bill Museum has an artifact donated by Elsa L. Schaffner which is a brass disc with a bullet dent used as a target in a demonstration by Annie Oakley at the Stone house in Amityville on August 9, 1909.

---

6   Fields, Armond, *Fred Stone, Circus Performer and Musical Comedy Star:* (McFarland & Company, Inc., 2002), 176.

7   Local Amityville history has it that Stone and Rogers were known to make frequent horseback rides to Loci's, the local confectionary, for cigars and candy with the local children running along with them.

8   Fields, 132

THE GOLDEN AVENUE

The following is from Shirl Kasper's biography of Annie Oakley:

> *They were there one day [the Butlers] when Fred, who was a baseball*
> *fan, came home with his team in tow. When the team decided to stay*
> *for lunch, Annie joined Allene and Fred's mother in the kitchen. While*
> *the women cooked, Fred gave a shooting exhibition on the lawn. The*
> *familiar pop of the shotgun attracted Annie's attention, and she came*
> *outside to see what was going on. "Can I have the shotgun for a minute?"*
> *she asked Fred, and he handed her the automatic shotgun. Frank*
> *threw up five targets in a bunch, and Annie, her hair shining white*
> *in the afternoon sun, gunned all five before they hit the ground.*
>
> *"Thanks, Fred," she said, and went back into the house.*
>
> *Mason Peters, a newspaper man in the group, couldn't believe what he'd seen.*
> *He mopped his head, turned to Stone and said, "My God, Fred, was that your*
> *mother?" Fred Stone loved to tell that story about Annie Oakley. "It was*
> *always amusing to watch people who were meeting her for the first time,"*
> *he said. "They expected to see a big, masculine, blustering sort of person,*
> *and the tiny woman with the quiet voice took them by surprise... There was*
> *never a sweeter, gentler, and more lovable woman than Annie Oakley."[9]*

In June of 1922 Fred Stone was planning a Motor Hippodrome and Wild West Show at the Mineola, L.I., race track to benefit the Occupational Therapy Society and he asked Annie to come and be the main attraction for the event. It was rumored that Oakley was considering a comeback and this would certainly have been a good opportunity to test the waters.

Stone was now in the motion picture business and he sent a western clad contingent,

---

9   Kasper, 188.

complete with a vintage stage coach[10] pulled by 4 mules to greet Annie at the Amityville train station and transport her to his home. The press made a big deal of this and Annie was warmly greeted by old and new fans when she led the parade at the July 1st event.

It was about this time, possibly after the benefit, that Annie and Frank Butler rented the house at 202 Ocean Avenue, about half way down, on the river side. It is said she kept her "animals" across the street on some vacant land. If she was, indeed, trying to restart her career she would have wanted to have her horses nearby. There is little information

10.2 A 1922 photo of Oakley likely taken at the Mineola Wild West Show.

available about this time in Annie's life. We know that she appeared at the Brockton, MA, fair in October of 1922 , her first paid performance in years, and she was delighted in her fee, $700 each for 5, five minute performances.[11] Perhaps attractive enough to pull the trigger on her comeback.

We will never know. On November 9, 1922 Annie and Frank were in a car accident on their way to winter in Florida. Annie's leg was badly broken and she spent six weeks in a Florida hospital. She would spend the rest of her days in a leg brace. Whatever hopes she had of a comeback were gone.

---

10   The 1832 stage coach was a gift from Joseph Kennedy to Fred Stone. Before his posting as Ambassador to England, Kennedy had been in the movie business. Stone subsequently gave the stage coach to his friend Will Rogers who eventually donated it to the Smithsonian Institution.

11   Kasper, 227

Annie and Frank never returned to Amityville. With failing health Annie and Frank moved back to Ohio to be close to Annie's family. In 1926, knowing her time was close, Annie sent her favorite saddle as a gift to Fred Stone's eldest daughter, Dorothy. Then on November 3, 1926, while traveling with a show, Fred received a trunk filled with Annie Oakley's press clippings and memorabilia and an unfinished autobiography.[12] She had named Fred Stone as executor. She died two days later.

---

12   Fields, 234.

CHAPTER 11- WALTER O'MALLEY AND THE DODGERS

In 1957 Ocean Avenue resident Walter O'Malley moved the Brooklyn Dodgers to Los Angeles and became the most hated man in Brooklyn. Michael D'Antonio opens his book *Forever Blue*, the story of O'Malley and his Dodgers, with this: "'He' was Walter O'Malley, the team's owner, and what he did would go down in history as a betrayal equal, in some minds, to Benedict Arnold's treason at West Point. At a time when people in Brooklyn were fighting to hold onto their optimism and identity, O'Malley uprooted the most important symbol of their plucky spirit and moved it to LA."[1] He may still be the most hated man in Brooklyn, but the story is not so simple and O'Malley not your standard villain.

O'Malley's tie to Amityville started as a child with the family's seasonal retreat from Brooklyn to their Ocean Avenue summer home. Walter's father, Edwin, was a member of the Tammany Hall gang in New York, holding the position of commissioner of markets, where he oversaw the licensing and operation of public markets in Manhattan. The Ocean Avenue home was one of three contiguous and identical structures built around 1905 as summer rentals. The three waterfront properties were numbers 298, 308 and 318 with the O'Malleys summering at 318. This was near the site of the earlier Ocean Point Hotel which

---

1   D'Antonio, Michael, *Forever Blue: The Story of Walter O'Malley, Baseball's Most Controversial Owner, and The Dodgers of Brooklyn and Los Angeles*. (Riverbed Books, New York, 2009), 2.

was destroyed by fire around 1900. The hotel was not rebuilt and the property sold off for residential development. The Mortimer Palmer House, built in 1907 on the former hotel property, was the last structure on Ocean Avenue's east side and just three houses down from the O'Malley summer home.

It was here that O'Malley fell in love with the girl next door, Katherine "Kay" Hanson, whose family summered next door at 308 Ocean Avenue. D'Antonio had access to O'Malley's correspondence and references a note from young Walter to Kay with "...lines to sensitive descriptions of the setting moon and signs of spring in coastal Amityville, including birds' nests, tulips, lilacs, schooling fish, and lavender blooming near the back door at the Hanson house."[2] He was obviously smitten.

The relationship grew and was tested when Kay was diagnosed with throat cancer. Walter's father suggested he sever the relationship but Walter walked out on his father, instead. He put himself through law school at Fordham University and set up practice in Brooklyn, specializing in contract law. Walter and Kay were married in 1931.

Kay struggled with the cancer all her life and, as a result of the surgeries, was not able to speak beyond a murmur, only intelligible to her closest family. I still remember trick-or-treating at their house; she would silently greet us with a warm smile and a treat. About the only sign of wealth at their home was the in-ground pool Walter had installed which the doctors prescribed as therapy for Kay's cancer.

Walter and Kay set up house in an apartment in the Crown Heights section of Brooklyn and Walter set about building his legal business and developing his business and political capital in Brooklyn. Following his mother's death in 1940, Walter began spending more time at the Ocean Avenue house with his aging father. Following his father's death in 1950 O'Malley moved the family to Amityville. The 2016 photo is of the Hanson house on the left and the O'Malley house on the right. As built, they were identical but Kay fancied

---

2   Ibid, 27.

11.1 The Hanson house is on the left and the O'Malley house on the right in 2016. It is hard to believe they were identical when built in 1905.

Frank Lloyd Wright's "Falling Waters" and the house was altered to reflect Wright's Prairie Modern look. It stood out as the only modern design on a street of traditional Victorian, Colonial Revival and Federal style homes.

We see an early relationship with George V. "The Fifth" McLaughlin, head of the Brooklyn Trust Bank.[3] McLaughlin and O'Malley were two of a politically connected group of Brooklyn Club members that met weekly for a poker game in the "coal hole" (basement) of the club. The Brooklyn Club was, and is, an exclusive social club for influential Brooklynites. It was through his relationship with McLaughlin that O'Malley

---

3   The Brooklyn Trust Bank was one of the five most influential banks in New York and a favorite of Robert Moses for underwriting his "authority" bond issues. McLaughlin was an ex-Tammany Hall politician who had not lost his political skills or contacts and was a close confidant of Robert Moses. He sat on the board of Robert Moses' Triborough Bridge and Tunnel Authority (TBTA), appointed by New York City Mayor LaGuardia.

was first introduced to the Dodgers. The Brooklyn Trust Bank held the mortgage for the Dodger's Ebbets Field and the team did not have a strong financial record. McLaughlin had brought Larry McPhail in to manage the team in 1938 but he needed someone to oversee the front office side of the business, so O'Malley was hired by McLaughlin to manage their contracts and business arrangements thus protecting the bank's investment.

In the 1860s Brooklyn boasted 100 baseball teams which seemed appropriate for their size; following the annexation of the Williamsburg and Bushwick areas, Brooklyn was the third largest city in America. The 1850s and '60s saw activity to create uniform rules and a formal baseball league. The National Association of Baseball Players League was formed in1858; the National League had 202 teams representing 17 states and the District of Columbia.[4]

The Brooklyns, the team that would become the Dodgers, was formed in 1883 in the shade of the newly opened Brooklyn Bridge. It is ironic that the bridge would end up playing a significant role in the story of the Dodgers' move to LA. In 1888 the team name was changed to the Bridegrooms or "Grooms," a reference to the number of ball players that were married in the previous off-season. 1888 was also the year the Giants started playing at the Polo Grounds and the first playing of an all-star game between the best of Brooklyn and the best of New York. New York won, beginning a century long tradition of the great rivalry between the Dodgers and the Giants and of the Dodgers routinely losing to their up-town rivals.

1898 was a significant year for both the team and the city. Charlie Ebbets, having worked for the team since its inception, took control of the ball club and Brooklyn, along with Queens and Staten Island, were merged into New York City. Not that Brooklyn was a willing participant. The Brooklyn Bridge was conceived in the mid 1800s as a way to provide expansion for New York City which was considered completely built-out. The

---

4   Goldstein, Richard, *Superstars and Screwballs: 100 Years of Brooklyn Baseball*, (A Dutton Book, New York), 5.

11.2 1890s team photo of the Brooklyns.

bridge was so named because it provided access to Brooklyn from crowded Manhattan Island. The irony was that new steel technology was required to build the bridge and that technology would later allow New York City to go vertical, making the bridge, in hindsight, unnecessary. The sad story for Brooklyn was that the bridge did just what it was intended to do, encourage New Yorkers to move to Brooklyn. The explosive growth following the 1883 bridge opening put a great strain on Brooklyn's ability to provide infrastructure to support the new population. Brooklyn went broke. New York City's offer to include Brooklyn was one they couldn't refuse. The third largest city in the nation was now just a part of the largest city in the nation. This would be the first step in the erosion of Brooklyn's unique identity- the loss of the Dodgers would be the last and the hardest of all.

11.3 The Brooklyn Bridge in a 1908 postcard.

1941 was a strong year for the team with attendance at one million compared to the league average of 550,000. General Manager McPhail had recruited Leo Durocher as manager and with O'Malley watching the business side, things were looking good. The Dodgers won the National League pennant with the star power of Joe DiMaggio and Ted Williams and faced the Yankees in the World Series.[5] This was a far cry from the woeful Dodgers of the 1930s that prompted cartoonist Willard Mullins to create the "Brooklyn Bum." The fans greeted the iconic character warmly and reveled in the attitude that "They may be bums but they're OUR bums."

Branch Rickey was hired as General Manager in 1942 and brought strength in player development and management. He would become a great champion of change and a major factor in Dodger lore. As early as 1943 Rickey met with George McLaughlin to

---

5   The Yankees won the series 4-1 in a near sweep.

broach the subject of bringing a black player into the league. McLaughlin gave his blessing and O'Malley was used as a scout; he was not officially part of the Dodger organization so would not attract attention to the activity. Rickey's recruitment of Jackie Robinson would become legendary while O'Malley's significant involvement, eventually as club majority owner, went unnoticed.

O'Malley continued to work for McLaughlin and the Dodgers through the war years. In 1944, with Brooklyn Trust backing, O'Malley joined with Branch Rickey and a third party to buy a 25% ownership in the team. Then in 1945 O'Malley bought out the Ebbets family 50% share. Rickey was named club President and O'Malley, Vice President of the Board. Rickey handled the player side and O'Malley the financial and operations side.[6] The other 25% was owned by James Mulvey who maintained a hostile position, especially to Rickey. In 1950 O'Malley bought the outstanding 25% share. It was also in 1950 that Branch Rickey started looking for a buyer for his share of the club. When no deal could be struck O'Malley stepped in and matched the outstanding offer and took over ownership of the team. It was not common knowledge that Rickey was in financial trouble, forcing that sale. He ended up resigning from the Dodgers and relocating to Pittsburg to manage the Pirates. O'Malley was accused of forcing him out but kept silent to protect Rickey's privacy.

Up until the mid-forties the Brooklyns- then Grooms then Superbas then Dodgers-had not always been competitive. In sixty seasons they had appeared in only 3 World Series and lost them all. And this when the National League only had 8 teams! The O'Malley/Rickey team set out to change that by addressing both the player and business sides of the endeavor with the most notable action the recruiting of Jackie Robinson to the franchise. Robinson spent two years with the Montreal Royals, the Dodgers' minor league team, then debuted with the Dodgers on April 15, 1947. The story of the first black player in major league baseball is both difficult and heart-warming as a "warts and all" tale of

---

6   D'Antonia, 86.

deep seated prejudice and the road to social justice in America.

With Rickey on board the Dodgers won 87 games in 1945, then 96 games in 1946, losing the pennant in the last game of the season to the Cardinals. "Dem Bums" were anything but. With the addition of Jackie Robinson to the roster in 1947 the team just got stronger, finishing with a record of 94-62 and a trip to the World Series. This would be the first of 6 fabled "subway" series between the Dodgers and Yankees from 1947 to 1956. The Dodgers lost them all except in 1955 when the cry of "wait 'til next year" was the Yankee wail. And the Yankees delivered on the promise, beating the Dodgers in 6 games in the 1956 World Series, their last as Brooklyn Dodgers.

But all was not fine in Flatbush. The post-war years were troubling for baseball in general and more so for the Dodgers. Major League Baseball was under fire from the Feds as they reviewed the 1922 anti-trust exclusion for baseball which permitted the "reserve clause," keeping players from negotiating with other teams. The owners had agreed to keep the number of franchises to 16 despite strong interest from non-northeastern cities, especially in California. This monopoly power had increased team revenues but held player salaries stagnant. At the same time, television ownership had exploded along with televised games and attendance at baseball parks was on the decline. All the owners were watching the successful moves of the Boston Braves to Milwaukee and the Philadelphia Athletics to Kansas City. They had huge new ball parks and the local support for mediocre performing teams was outstanding. O'Malley was quoted, "[that positive experience]…could be duplicated in about any part of the country where an urban population is surrounded by solid suburban communities and where people travel mostly by automobile."[7]

The plight of the Dodgers was more troubling. Ebbets Field was over 40 years old and only held 32,000, the second smallest ball field in the majors, and it only had 700 parking

---

7   D'Antonio, 205.

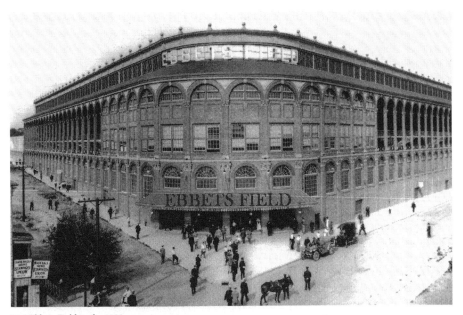

11.4 Ebbets Field in the 1920s

spaces. It was out of step with the post-war "age of the automobile." Despite strong team performance years in Brooklyn, attendance was soft. Even with Jackie Robinson and a pennant winning team in 1947, attendance was only up eleven thousand over the previous year. From their best attendance year in 1947 (1.8 million) fan support would fall even in World Series years- 1949, 1.6 million, 1952, 1.1 million, 1953, 1.2 million, 1955, 1.0 million, 1956, 1.2 million.[8] 1952 was especially depressing with a loss of two hundred thousand in attendance and 5,000 empty seats for game 5 of the World Series against the Yankees.

The Dodgers faced a significant post-war change in urban demographics with southern blacks moving north for economic opportunity and returning white servicemen leaving Brooklyn for suburban Long Island. The traditional Dodgers fan base- white,

---

8   www.baseball-reference.com/teams/LAD, referenced 3/30/17

male, 18 to 28 years old- was eroding. At the same time, Robert Moses was running New York City's urban renewal program that ended up displacing a large part of the City's lower income population who were forced to find new housing; many ended up in nearby Brooklyn. Despite Jackie Robinson's success and the growing number of blacks on the roster, new black fans were not compensating for the loss of white ticket holders. With both radio and television coverage of the games, it was easier to stay home. D'Antonio observed, "Eventually the middle-class march to the suburbs that began after World War II would be recognized as a major factor in the transformation of urban neighborhoods across the country. But this dynamic wasn't named, quantified, or even recognized in the beginning. All that the Dodgers management knew was that while they put their best team in the league on the field, they weren't keeping up with the competition at the gate."[9]

As early as 1946, O'Malley, realizing that Ebbets Field was not going to take the Dodgers where they wanted to go, began the process of looking for a new home. He started with architect Emil Praeger, a favorite of Robert Moses, to review the Ebbets Field site for possible renovation and expansion. Praeger's verdict was not optimistic. They were going to need a new stadium.

As attendance flagged, O'Malley started to get serious about a new stadium in 1951 when he met with city officials to start the process. In August he invited a critical group to join him at Ebbets Field for the annual "Music Depreciation Night." D'Antonio notes, "The only thing, or to be precise, important person- missing from the celebration that August night was Robert Moses, who O'Malley had hoped would join him, Impy [New York Mayor Vincent Impellitteri] and Cashmere [borough president John Cashmere] in the owner's box. No one was more important when it came to O'Malley's plans for a future stadium, and for the future of the Dodgers. Moses, who was hardly the type to enjoy cheering with thousands of working-class Brooklynites, had agreed to come to the

---

9   D'Antonio, 114

game but then cancelled. By the time O'Malley came along, Moses was more powerful than any elected official in the state, including the mayor and the governor. He operated beyond oversight and was immune to the will of the voters. Anyone who thought to build anything with government help in New York only needed Moses to make it happen. Of course, the opposite was true too: if Moses didn't want your project, it died."[10]

The next five years would see a frustrated O'Malley try again and again to get Moses behind his new stadium. O'Malley had found a location in the Fort Greene area of Brooklyn and needed Moses' help to get it, first, condemned, then financed through the Federal Title I process. The site would support the stadium, parking, new public housing and a new Long Island Railroad terminal. Following a meeting in 1955 with New York City Mayor John Wagner, borough president John Cashmere, O'Malley and Moses, all Moses agreed to was a study of the concept. Moses had doubts about whether building a stadium for a private entity would qualify for public money, even when the project included public housing and a train station, although Moses never let minor details like that get in his way before. "In the crosscurrents of New York Politics, the enthusiasms of Robert Moses mattered more than almost anything. The big challenge, of course, was in determining which way they were running. As much as O'Malley detractors would complain that he was inscrutable and scheming, compared with Moses he was a political amateur. At the start of 1956, Moses told an aide that he had already decided against helping O'Malley build in Brooklyn. However, he added, "It is necessary to show that our opposition is based on something other than prejudice.""[11]

There is an interesting quote from Moses about Brooklyn and the Dodgers made at an address to the Pratt Institute in 1955. He was mourning the loss of the *Brooklyn Eagle*, Brooklyn's only real newspaper. "If only a fraction of the genuine enthusiasm which the

---

10   Ibid, 154.

11   Ibid, 230.

Dodgers arouse could be channeled into building a new Brooklyn, what a town that would be! When the Dodgers are on top it's the morning's morning in Flatbush and all Brooklyn believes that God's in His heaven and all's right in the world. When the Dodgers are down, there is no joy in Gowanus, no balm in Gravesend and the shades are drawn on the old Canarsie farm. What a people! Happy or blue, their disposition depends on the standing of the team."[12]

Along the way Moses suggested a site in Queens to which O'Malley grunted "We are the Brooklyn Dodgers, not the Queens Dodgers." Lacking public support the suggestion died. That property eventually became the site of Shea Stadium in 1962, the home of the New York Mets.

In 1956 Moses reversed his position on Title I appropriateness and proposed the creation of the Brooklyn Sports Center Authority which would build the public stadium and rent it back to the Dodgers. He would require the Dodgers buy $5 Million in Authority Bonds. O'Malley agreed but the project went nowhere. O'Malley had sold Ebbets Field with a commitment to the new owners to play there for the '56 and '57 seasons so something had to happen. It was obvious this had been a Moses stalling tactic.

O'Malley wasn't stupid and had considered moving the team to California as early as 1949. His first choice was to build and own a stadium in Brooklyn. He would even consider a publicly owned stadium in Brooklyn even though multi-use stadiums were notoriously bad for baseball and baseball fans. California was itching to get into baseball now that air travel made it possible for West Coast teams to participate. Representatives of Los Angeles and San Francisco were quite noisy in their maneuvering to entice teams, especially competitive teams, to their cities. On opening day at Ebbets Field in 1957 only 11,000 fans showed up. As of the May 1957 National League meeting the Dodgers were formally allowed to consider a move but a Brooklyn Stadium was still technically alive.

---

12   Ibid, 211.

Walter O'Malley and the Dodgers

Moses was quoted in the July 1957 issue of *Sports Illustrated* saying that the stadium would not happen and blamed it all on O'Malley. Up until then O'Malley was fending off LA's advances but quickly got serious. A National League rule kept teams from announcing a move until October 1st and then they had only three weeks to do so. On October 7, 1957 LA's offer was made and accepted by the Dodgers. They would open their 1958 season at the Los Angeles Coliseum.

Walter O'Malley later reflected about Robert Moses. "As to friendship, Bob and I knew each other over a long span of years and we were very close. Bob became an enemy when he sabotaged our plans to build a stadium in Brooklyn. He became a benefactor when his opposition became so violent that we left Brooklyn and happily became established in California."[13]

The opening of the Brooklyn Bridge began the slow and painful process of identity loss for the citizens of Brooklyn. They watched as Brooklyn became a subset of New York City in 1898, as the Brooklyn Navy Yard, their largest employer (70,000 during the war) faded to 10,000 jobs then closed in 1966, as the Brooklyn Trust Bank was merged out of business and the *Brooklyn Eagle*, once the largest daily in the country, stopped its presses in 1955. Losing the Dodgers was the final blow.

The move to LA was the cover story in *Time Magazine* for their April 28, 1958 issue. The stilted piece was preceded by an unflattering photo of O'Malley on the cover and their unique brand of "death by pejorative adjective" journalism. Consider the first two sentences. "The man with the ample jowls swiveled happily in his chair. Cigar ash dribbled over his shirt front, and his several chins bobbled as his tight little mouth widened into a smile."[14] Perhaps an attempt to portray O'Malley more as a Tammany Hall politician, like his father, than an astute business man. Just after Charlie Ebbets took over

---

13   Ibid, 340.

14   "Walter in Wonderland," *Time Magazine*, April 28, 1958, 58

the team in 1898 he was asked by the press if he was going to build a new field to replace the original Washington Park. He retorted, "The question is purely one of business. I am not in baseball for my health."[15] Neither was Walter O'Malley.

It is interesting that following the team's move to L.A. the O'Malleys stayed in Amityville. Kay loved the area and hated to leave her non-baseball friends. Walter ran the business from the east coast with his son Peter taking on increasing responsibility in the organization. Walter turned over the presidency to Peter in 1970 and stepped back to Chairman of the Board. It wasn't

11.5 Time Magazine, April 28, 1958.

until the 1970s that Walter and Kay moved to California, we assume, more for climate and family than team.

* *

Now, sixty years later, we have a less emotional view of the battle. The loss to metropolitan New York baseball was dramatic especially when you remember that O'Malley was able to convince the New York baseball Giants to relocate to San Francisco the same year. They played each other on opening day 1958 starting a new, West Coast,

---

15   Goldstein, 354.

rivalry. This time the Dodgers won.

D'Antonio sums up O'Malley's contribution this way. "Under O'Malley a strong, stable Dodger franchise continued the racial progress begun by Branch Rickey. He sparked unequaled growth in his industry and created wealth that was evenly distributed far more equitably to players, managers, and coaches of all races and backgrounds. Walter O'Malley's truth, while painful for Brooklyn, made the game thrive in ways that benefitted millions of fans while he lived, and millions more after he died." [16]

Walter O'Malley died on August 9, 1979 less than a year before his induction into the National Baseball Hall of Fame, Cooperstown, N.Y., in July of 1980.

But the locals will never forget. Goldstein recounts a 1990 interview he had with Tom Knight, Brooklyn's historian for baseball, 33 years after the Dodgers left. Knight's job had been to keep the memories alive. He recounted:

> *"A guy says to me, 'How could a man from Brooklyn do a thing like that?'*
>
> *I said, 'Well, he wasn't from Brooklyn. He came from Amityville.'*
>
> *Knight pauses then comes to the punch line, delivered with gusto, 'He was the original Amityville Horror.'"* [17]

---

16   D'Antonio, 345.

17   Goldstein, 358.

CHAPTER 12- THE GAMBLINGS OF WOR RADIO

In 1925 John B. Gambling was a recently arrived New Yorker and looking for work. He was a British citizen originally headed for a career in horticulture but fascinated with early radio because of the sinking of the Titanic and the role the telegraph played in that disaster. He served in the Royal Navy as a wireless operator during WWI and took that skill to the merchant shipping business after the war and then to an ocean liner where he met and married his American wife. She convinced him to look for a job on dry land, in the United States, and he ended up at the fledgling WOR Radio in New York City.

12.1 John B. Gambling, 1945

WOR was the second radio station in New York, having started in 1922 just behind WJZ, founded a year earlier. In 1925 there were only 3 million radio receivers in the whole country[1] but the future for radio looked bright. Westinghouse was so successful selling $10 receivers they decided to get into the radio station business to create programming for their customers, an interesting reverse to the "razors and blades" marketing strategy popular in the 1950s and beyond.

Gambling started at WOR as a station engineer but on a fateful day in early 1925 the celebrated Bernarr Macfadden, of health and fitness fame, failed to show for his morning radio exercise program. Gambling was pressed into service (he may have been the only one at the station at the time). His expertise was with the dots and dashes of Morse Code but he sucked it up and filled the hour-long spot with instruction and exercise cadence. His mellow voice and reassuring tone was a hit with the listeners and he soon replaced Macfadden as the morning host of what became "Gambling's Musical Clock." He created his own format of news headlines, personal chatter and live music which became the "Rambling With Gambling" show in 1942.

He was such a fixture on WOR that 27,000 fans showed up at the 30th anniversary special broadcast from Madison Square Garden in 1955 to wish him well. And all this for a morning segment when folks were just getting out of bed and finding their way to work.

Getting Up in the Morning

• John B. Gambling, WOR's popular announcer, is heard each morning except Sundays directing the early morning exercises, which is sponsored by Clemens, Inc., Men's tailors. He wanted to be a horticulturist and spent his adolescent days in Cambridge, England, studying horticulture. He entered the mercantile marine and became chief operator on the big passenger ships. John liked America so well that he entered his name on the quota list and after arriving, was given a position on the engineering staff of WOR. Soon it was found that he had a microphone personality and was shifted to the announcer's staff.

12.2 From a 1931 issue of *Radio Guide*, the forerunner to TV Guide

---

1   Hinckley, David, *John B. Gambling's rise from fill-in to NYC's first radio star*, New York Daily News, 8/14/2017.

He was like family.

You could easily title this story "British boy makes good in America; radio comes of age," and move on. But stay tuned, the fun had just begun.

The Gamblings were Long Island people and had lived in Nassau Shores in Massapequa and Merrick before moving to Ocean Avenue in the 1940s.[2] Their son, John A. Gambling, took to the water like his dad, but also took to radio just like his dad. In 1959 John B. retired from WOR Radio and passed along the Rambling With Gambling program to 29 year-old John A. Dad had established a very popular format and John A. continued the success without skipping a beat. He tweaked the program a bit, doing away with the music and adding more talk and a news helicopter, but kept the folksy and friendly personal chatter. He was labeled a "warm hearted optimist" and avoided controversy on air while his competition were looking for edgy issues. He was quoted as saying, "I believe the morning is bad enough as it is." Most New Yorkers seemed to agree.

During his reign a 1985 article in *People Magazine* captured the essence of his success, "His fans don't ask for an autograph; they invite him for lunch."[3] He was family. John A. was elected to the Radio Hall of Fame in 2000.

But the story just gets better. John A. retired from WOR in 1991 after 32 years on the air. He wanted to pursue his passion for sailing, nurtured those many summers growing up on the Great South Bay. Amid cries of nepotism, again, he passed along the Rambling With Gambling show to his 41 year-old son John R. Gambling. John R. had spent a number of years as his dad's co-host and moved easily into the role with little change other than a bit more opinion than dad and granddad. John R. took the show to the year 2000, completing an unprecedented 75 years on the air for the three John Gamblings. The

2   Amityville Historical Society, *Images of America: Amityville*, (Arcadia Publishing, Charleston, South Carolina. 2006,) 100.

3   Kahn, Toby, *John B. Gambling Begat John A. Who Begat John R. and That's How Radio's Oldest Dynasty Was Born*, People Magazine, 1/28/1985.

The Gamblings of WOR Radio

Guiness Book of World Records proclaimed it the longest running radio program.[4]

By 2000 the homey, conservative format was mainly attracting older listeners that did not fit the target profile of many of the radio advertisers. John R. and the iconic show was cancelled so he took his morning show across town to rival WABC but was wooed back to WOR in 2008. His final broadcast was in 2013 when the last of the radio Gamblings hung up his microphone for good.

An interesting side note to the Gambling story is that fellow radio broadcaster for WOR Radio, Henry Gladstone, lived across the street from the Gamblings on Ocean Avenue[5] during the 1940s and 50s.

Gladstone was a Boston boy, educated at the University of Toronto and an aspiring thespian as a young man. His few off-Broadway roles did not promise a path to stardom so he moved into the New York radio scene starting with WOR in 1942 and retiring from the station in 1977. Along the way he established his credentials as a first-rate newsman, first as one of WOR's *News-On-The-Hour* anchors then as their United Nations correspondent. Many remember him as the narrator for the *March of Times* newsreels during World War II.

We do not know who was first to Ocean Avenue and if either Gambling or Gladstone had any influence on the other. And with their conflicting program schedules it is likely they would only bump into each other at the annual Christmas party.

Just maybe, they simply shared a love of Sundays on the bay.

---

4   Since then, The Grand Ol' Opry has eclipsed *Rambling with Grambling's* 75 years.

5   Amityville Historical Society, *Images of America: Amityville*, (Arcadia Publishing, Charleston, South Carolina. 2006), 100.

Chapter 13- Ed Nezbeda and Grumman

Aviation in America may have been born in Dayton, Ohio, but it spent its infancy and adolescence on Long Island. While the Wright Brothers were trying to get the patent rights to anything pertaining to flying, Long Islanders were busy inventing flying machines and establishing early production companies of their own.

In 1909 Frank VanAnden of Islip flew the first Long Island built airplane, followed quickly by Francois and Bessica Raiche of Mineola who built a plane in their backyard. Bessica was the first woman in America to build and fly an airplane. Lawrence Sperry, at the age of 17, was right on their heels with the plane he built in Brooklyn and flew from the Sheepshead Bay race track in 1910.

By the start of World War I Long Island had hosted eighteen new airplane tests and start-up companies. By the end of the war that number grew to twenty seven including such notables as Willard-Curtiss, Moisant Aeroplane, Lawrence Sperry Aircraft Corporation, Loening Aeronautical Engineering Corporation, Chance Vaught Corporation and Curtiss Aeroplane and Motor Corporation.

Long Island combined a number of factors that made it the ideal place for early aviation to grow and prosper. First, Hempstead Plain was the only natural prairie east of the Allegheny Mountains[1] which made for flat runways and easy, treeless, low flying.

---

1   Stoff, Joshua, *Long Island Aircraft and Manufacturers:* (Arcadia Publishing, Charleston, South Carolina, 2010), 7.

Add to this the proximity of New York's capital markets, good roads and rail service, an abundance of skilled labor and an eager and well trained immigrant labor pool- together they made a great recipe for the development of the early aeronautic industry.

It is surprising that although the emergence of military aircraft was a huge contributor to the end of World War I, the United States military did little to promote aircraft development following the war. This was not true of European nations, especially France and Germany. While the U.S. military was doing little to encourage war plane development the number of nascent aircraft manufacturers was on the rise. By the time of Lindberg's historic flight in 1927 the number of Long Island aircraft start-ups was up to forty-one, many looking to supply the mail service or the slow growing private and commercial markets.

The market crash and start of the Depression in 1929 thinned the field of Long Island aircraft aspirants but many new entrants appeared. Sikorsky (1923) and Fairchild (1925) survived the crash and were joined by fledgling Grumman (1930), Seversky[2] (1932) and Brewster (1932). The stirring winds of World War II would stimulate aircraft development despite the publicly stated goal of neutrality for the United States. We had lost ground after World War I and there was much catching up to do.

* *

Grumman Aircraft Engineering Corporation

The Grumman story is truly an American success story. Three Loening Aeronautical Engineering employees, led by Leroy Grumman, struck off on their own when Loening was merged with Keystone Aviation in 1928 and operations were to be moved to Bristol,

---

2   Seversky would reorganize in 1939 to become Republic Aviation.

PA "...which marked the edge of outer space to anyone living in the New York area..."[3] Starting up in January of 1930 with a focus on product, people and superior engineering, they would prosper through the worst depression the country had ever known. The early goal was a diversified product portfolio built around superior aluminum fabrication technology but the looming war and their aeronautic upbringing drew them into a close relationship with the U. S. Navy. By the end of World War II Grumman was the largest employer on Long Island, with a high of 25,000 workers contributing to the war effort.

Grumman began with about 18 former Loening Aircraft employees, no external capital, no products and no orders. They did start with a hand-picked group of skilled aircraft factory workers and some strategies grown from their former work at Loening. To pay the bills and survive their first year they planned to buy and repair crashed Loening aircraft- skills they had as they had built the planes in the first place.

Roy Grumman also brought with him the knowledge of Navy interest in a float design with retractable wheels for their Vought Corsair amphibious fighters that would allow land, sea and carrier landings, improving the plane's versatility. Grumman's strategy included diversified products such as aluminum truck bodies but becoming an approved supplier to the Navy for the floats would put them on the road to designing an airplane, their ultimate strategic goal.

The float design presented to the Navy included stressed skin technology and retractable landing gear: the combination produced a lighter float than in current use even with the addition of the retractable landing gear mechanism. The Navy liked what they saw and ordered two in February of 1930. The new float did everything it promised- added function to the Vought Corsair fighters, reduced overall weight and increased speed and range. The Grumman design became Navy Float Type A and the resulting orders filled the new venture's first assembly line.

---

3   Thruelsen, Richard, *The Grumman Story*, (Praeger Publishers, New York, 1976), 18

The Navy was so impressed with the Grumman effort, and their retractable wheel design, they asked if Grumman could retrofit the current Navy fighter to include retractable landing gear. They were ready for the question and responded that the current fighter design did not have sufficient space in the fuselage to accommodate the retracted wheels. However, Grumman would be happy to quote their own design for a fighter incorporating the retractable wheels. The Navy agreed.

13.1 First flight of the XFF-1, Grumman's first experimental fighter. Photo courtesy of the Grumman Historic Center

Navy plane requirements were distinct from those of the Army because they included aircraft carrier landings and takeoffs requiring slow speed maneuverability and a high climb rate as well as greater structural integrity. The Navy liked the plans and ordered the experimental two-seat fighter on March 6, 1931 with the designation X(experimental) F(fighter)F(the Grumman designation)-1. Grumman referred to it as "the plane."

The bi-wing XFF-1 tested in December of '31 and even with the retracted landing gear was faster than the current Navy single-seater fighter, though the fuselage design was less svelte. The gang at the factory called her "Fertile Myrtle." During development of the

13.2 Postcard view of the single-seater F2F

fighter the Navy also asked Grumman to quote a scout version of the plane that would replace the armament with an extra gas tank for extended reconnaissance missions. In December of 1932 the Navy accepted the XFF-1 and ordered 27 for delivery in 1933. Later that year the scout

13.3 The Grumman F3F, the last of the bi-wing fighters.

version was also approved and 33 were ordered for delivery in the first half of 1934.

This very rapid growth resulted in a November, 1931, move from their start-up location in Baldwin, Long Island, to a larger factory in nearby Valley Stream. They moved again the next year to Farmingdale, Long Island, when production orders for both planes were anticipated. At that time they needed assembly areas for the Navy floats, truck bodies, fighters and scouts and room for additional development programs.

By 1934, with the success of both the FF-1 two-seat fighter and the FS-1 scout, the Navy asked the logical question, "How much better could a single-seat fighter be?" Development began on the bi-wing XF2F and it tested at 250 MPH, out-performing all Air Corps fighters despite the restrictions of carrier based operations. The Navy ordered 55 and a fourth production line was started in 1935. The five year old company was on a roll.

It was in 1934 that Roy Grumman is quoted as saying "I never want this company to get over two hundred and fifty employees. When it does it's going to be too big and

13.4 The Grumman Goose

we are going to lose control of it. That's where we ought to stop."[4] Clint Towl, his chief

production guy at the time, had to tell him they were already at 266. Roy Grumman would

continue to be concerned about the company's manageability as the 'tiger by the tail'

relationship with the Navy took Grumman employment to 25,000 by the end of the war.

Staying small was not an option.

During 1934 Grumman developed the F3F, fixing a few issues with the F2F including

a bigger engine. In August of 1935 the Navy ordered 54 planes and Grumman had it's

first million dollar order. A second order for 81 planes in March of 1936 prompted

Grumman's third and final move to Bethpage where the first production line was

completed in April of 1937. Grumman produced the bi-wing F3F until May of 1939 when

it was replaced by the first monoplane design, just in time for our entry into World War II.

---

4   Ibid, 80

Despite Grumman's success with the Navy they continued to develop aircraft for non-military use realizing that an all-military product line would put the corporation in a difficult position. In 1937 they flew the first test flight of the Goose (G21), an early attempt at a corporate aircraft. The Goose was a boat-hull, high wing amphibian with seating for eight plus two crew members. Although the target was the commercial market, their largest customer turned out to be the Coast Guard. Grumman would always have an affinity for amphibian aircraft and end up producing this style plane in four sizes- the Widgeon, the Mallard, the Goose and the Albatross.

1939 saw the development of the first single-wing, monoplane design, designated the F4F. This "Wildcat" would be the first of the Grumman "cats" and mark the most significant aircraft development for World War II. The Navy ordered 54 F4F-3 planes for delivery in 1940 then, anticipating hostile activity and to fulfill Lend-Lease commitments, ordered an additional 759 fighters in 1940 to be built at Plant #2 in Bethpage. Congress

Grumman F4F-3-U. S. Navy Fighter

13.5 The Grumman F4F Wildcat

passed the Engineering Plant Facilities Act in 1940 which made Federal funds available to contractors, such as Grumman, to get production facilities built quickly in preparation for war. As such, Plant #2 was Government owned but Grumman operated.[5] This duality would become an issue in the post-war years.

The large orders for Wildcats were to arm the carrier groups for activity in the Pacific. 1940 saw significant activity at Grumman to perfect the folding wing which would allow greater below deck storage on aircraft carriers. The innovative design put five aircraft in the space of two with wings unfolded, a significant achievement for the Navy. The first Wildcats to see action were in Great Britain before our entry in the war. Winston Churchill affectionately called the Wildcat the "scourge of the Atlantic."[6]

* *

Edward Nezbeda

Ed Nezbeda joined Grumman in 1940 with the permanent employee number 1101. He was a Linden, New Jersey boy, the first-generation American son of an immigrant father and mother from near Prague, what is now the Czech Republic. His father was a tool and die maker and owned his own machine shop. Ed grew up in a stern environment as evidenced by a story he liked to tell. As a teenager he was sent across town to pick up 100 pounds of parts for his father's machine shop and given a nickel for the trolley. When he reminded his father the trolley was five cents each way he was told to decide for himself the best way to spend the nickel.

Ed's father died in an automobile accident in 1936 and he was left to put himself through Newark College of Engineering where he graduated in 1939 with a degree in

---

5   Gunston, Bill, *Grumman: Sixty Years of Excellence*, (Orion Books, New York, 1988), 25

6   Ibid, 36

13.6 Ed Nezbeda's Grumman employee card. Photo courtesy the Grumman History Center

mechanical engineering. His first job was with Davis Engineering but within a year or so he joined Grumman in Bethpage and took a room at a boarding house on Dixon Avenue in Amityville with a number of other Grumman bachelors.

His timing couldn't have been better. Grumman was struggling to keep up with orders for the Wildcat and the Goose. They had impressed the Navy with their design engineering and prototyping but were now faced with the need to produce a large quantity of increasingly complex airplanes for the war effort. With his mechanical engineering skills Ed would be in the vanguard of the development of an industry leading manufacturing engineering department at Grumman.

Late in 1940 the Navy picked the Grumman design for a torpedo bomber to replace the Douglas TBD then in use. Although the Grumman prototype was not flown until August of 1941, the Navy had ordered 286 planes from the 1940 drawings, trusting the results of the test flight would be positive. They were. The manufacturing schedule was

13.7 Grumman TBF-1 torpedo bomber

getting loaded and we weren't officially in the war yet.

On Sunday, December 7th, 1941, Grumman was having an open house for the dedication of the newly completed Plant #2 in Bethpage. The plant was filled with workers and their families when telephone news of the attack on Pearl Harbor was received. The festivities were quietly ended and the plant was searched for saboteurs.[7] We were at war.

The Wildcat was the primary aircraft in early action in the Pacific. It was slower and less maneuverable than the Japanese Zero but kept us in the fight due to superior pilots and an airplane that could take a beating and still get its pilot home. The reliability of the Wildcat was so legendary Grumman became known as the "Iron Works" by the young pilots that flew them. During 1942 Grumman developed the F6F, a faster, more maneuverable fighter that would take the fight to the Japanese. It was called the Hellcat. 12,275 Hellcats were produced from 1943 to 1945. In their first air battle on December

---

7   Ibid, 40.

13.8 WWII pilots with a Grumman Hellcat in the background

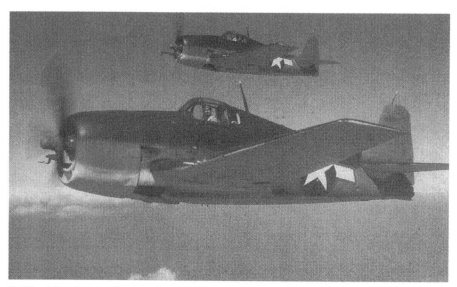

13.9 The Hellcat, introduced at the end of 1943, changed the course of the war in the Pacific.

Ed Nezbeda and Grumman

4th, 1943, 91 Hellcats met 50 Zeroes destroying 28 Zeroes and losing only 2 of their own. The Hellcat helped turn the tide of the war in the Pacific. For the entire war the Hellcat accounted for 5,155 confirmed kills of the total 6,477 enemy aircraft shot down.[8]

An early assignment for Ed Nezbeda was to help General Motors set up their plants in Linden and Elizabeth, New Jersey, to produce the Grumman torpedo bomber (TBF), designated the TBM for planes produced by the General Motors Eastern Aviation Division.[9] The Navy engineered this arrangement so Grumman could focus on production of the Hellcat. Nezbeda was picked for the job because manufacturing engineering was his forte and it didn't hurt that he could spend time with his Mother at her home in Linden, New Jersey. It was also convenient for Ed to kindle a romance with Blanche Kontur, also a first generation "New Jerseyite," whom he would marry in 1943 after his New Jersey stint was done. They bought a house on Bayview Avenue in Amityville and started their family before moving to Ocean Avenue in 1955.[10]

Nezbeda came back to Bethpage to help engineer the new Plant #3 for production of the Hellcat. By the end of the war Plant #3 was turning out 20 Hellcats a day- one airplane for each hour of daily plant operation. In 1986 the *New York Times* ran an article honoring Grumman and its Hellcat, reviewing an exhibit at the Smithsonian Institution's National Air and Space Museum. The article included this insight into employee relations at Grumman:

> Leroy and his partners regarded the employee as the key element
> in production. To combat what they considered "the enemies of

---

8   Ibid, 43.

9   On September 2, 1944 George H. Bush, Lieutenant JG, was shot down in the Pacific while flying a Grumman TBM produced at the Linden, NJ, Eastern Aviation plant.

10   Long time residents of Ocean Avenue tell of an anti-aircraft gun placement at the village dock at the foot of Ocean Avenue. It was feared that enemy bombers could use the Amityville river to point them directly to Republic Aviation in Farmingdale and Grumman in Bethpage.

production" - boredom, low morale and domestic worries- they
offered workers unusual benefits, including day-care centers staffed
with nurses for small children, musical entertainment during work
breaks, and production bonuses. A "Little Green Truck" ran errands
for employees, such as picking up packages or towing a worker's car.

At the peak of wartime production in 1943, Grumman
employed 25,527 workers, about a third of them women.
Five women were wartime test pilots.[11]

On August 8th, 1945, the United States dropped an atomic bomb on Hiroshima,
Japan. Following Japan's August 15th surrender a plant-wide announcement was made
over Grumman's loud speaker that all work was to stop and all 20,500 employees were laid
off. The Navy had cancelled all open orders. They were told that following an assessment
of labor requirements for post-war production, employees that were to be rehired would
be notified by telegram.[12] Three days later 5,400 employees got their telegrams. Ed
Nezbeda was one of them.

It is obvious that Nezbeda had good reason to be one of the rehires but he also
possessed a job skill that was acutely and immediately required. He could operate a
bulldozer. He arrived back at work at Plant #4 where a number of Hellcats sat on the
tarmac, wing tip to wing tip, ready for test flights and delivery. But there would be no
delivery. Ed's first job was to run a bulldozer up one wing, over the cockpit and down the
other wing, flattening each plane so they could be loaded on waiting flatbed trucks and
hauled to the scrap yard. He said that was the toughest job he ever had, destroying what
his team had worked so hard to build.

With the work force trimmed to a peace-time production level, Grumman set out to

---

11   http://www.nytimes.com/1986/01/05/nyregion/honoring-grumman-and-its-hellcat.html?mcubc=3

12   Skurla, George M. and Gregory, William H., *Inside The Iron Works*, (Naval Institute Press, Annapolis, Maryland, 2004), 25.

13.10 The Grumman Mallard

test its ability to prosper without the huge military demand for warplanes. Sales dropped from $236 million in 1945 to just $38 million in 1946 but they remained profitable. Military aircraft still represented the bulk of their business but with an emphasis on reconnaissance, utility transport, air/sea rescue and anti-submarine warfare. The Albatross was to be the most successful entry in these categories.

Grumman had not given up on the commercial market and the post-war slow down gave them the opportunity to complete designs for two light plane concepts, the Kitten (land based) and the Tadpole (amphibian). That market never materialized and neither of these planes was ever produced. However, Grumman was successful with the Mallard, a 12 passenger amphibian with application to the emerging corporate and up-scale private markets. Fifty-nine were produced through 1950.

The lean post-war years were followed by slow, measured growth as Grumman successfully competed for the nation's scaled down appetite for military aircraft. The last of the piston engined propellor aircraft for the Navy included the Hunter/Killer (AF-2S & AF-2W) duo of anti-submarine aircraft, replaced in the 1950s by the Tracker, a single, carrier based, aircraft with the same skill set in one aircraft. The development of the F9F Panther took Grumman to the jet age and the

13.11 The F9F Panther, Grumman's first jet aircraft.

swept-wing version, the Cougar, took them close to supersonic and kept them in the Navy fighter business albeit at peacetime volumes. The F11F was the next in the progression of fighters and their first supersonic fighter. It would be Grumman's last until the appearance

13.12 The E-2 Hawkeye

of the F14 Tomcat in 1972, the most sophisticated carrier based fighter ever produced and made even more famous by the movie *Top Gun*.

Filling out the production lines were a number of utility aircraft including the Mohawk, carry-it-all, do-it-all workhorse

13.13 A-6 Intruder

for the Army, the WF-2 Tracer, carrier based surveillance plane and the E-2 Hawkeye which replaced the Tracer, incorporating state-of-the-art surveillance technology. Grumman also supplied the Navy with the A-6 Intruder in many versions, most notably as a primary airborne attack weapons system.

It was during this period Ed Nezbeda prospered in the near meritocracy of

Ed Nezbeda and Grumman

Grumman. By 1955 he had advanced to chief tool engineer and was on the company's fast-track management development program. Following a management course at Cornell he spent time with the purchasing and accounting groups to round out his company base. In 1957 Nezbeda moved his family to Newton, MA, to become a Sloane Fellow at MIT, graduating the following year with a master's degree in industrial management. In 1964 he was elected corporate vice president and director of manufacturing engineering.

Ed Nezbeda got the top manufacturing job just in time to take Grumman to the next level in aircraft

13.14 Company portrait of Ed Nezbeda. Photo courtesy Kurt Nezbeda.

production. In early 1960 Grumman created a team to investigate the possibility of seeking a part of the Government's proposed Apollo space program. They were chosen to quote on the lunar module portion of the mission in 1962 and by 1967 there was a major shift from design and engineering to manufacturing. It fell to Nezbeda's group to build the 11 Lunar Modules (LMs) for testing and eventual moon landings. The LM was the most sophisticated aircraft Grumman ever built and the most critical in terms of performance and visibility. John F. Kennedy had set the goal of landing a man on the moon by the end of the decade.

In the summer of 1965 I found myself unexpectedly unemployed as the result of a union strike at a local aluminum ladder factory where I had found a summer job.

13.15 Buzz Aldrin and the Lunar Module on the Moon

Ed Nezbeda found out about my predicament and called right away to tell me I had a job at Grumman if I wanted it. I started the next day as a stock clerk at one of Grumman's warehouses in Bethpage. It was not exciting work- we received large quantities of stock small parts like nuts and bolts and grommets and "O" rings, then filled requisitions from the various plants. The only exciting day was when a camera for the LM arrived and we all envisioned handling something that would end up on the moon. Unfortunately, the camera was walked in, processed, and walked right out again. No Robinson fingerprints would find their way to the moon.

In all, eleven LMs were built for both testing and moon landings. Six are on the moon as testament to man's creative spirit and Grumman's engineering talents. Kurt Nezbeda tells the story of Saturday, January 28th, 1967. He was home for semester break from Bucknell and his dad suggested he join him at work saying "You might just learn something." They were out on the tarmac inspecting one of Grumman's planes when his dad learned of the fire at the Kennedy Space Center the day before, killing astronauts Gus Grissom, Ed White and Roger Chaffee. Ed Nezbeda knew all three astronauts personally from their training days at Bethpage in the LM simulator and Kurt could see him fighting back tears from the loss.

Our family moved back to Amityville in 1953. Kurt Nezbeda and I became fast friends in fourth grade. The Nezbedas moved to 328 Ocean Avenue in 1955 and our friendship grew, especially after their return from Newton, Mass. Their house, built just after the turn of the 20th Century, was three doors north of the Village Dock, two doors North of the Palmer House and next door to the O'Malley's. The spacious four bedroom house had an over-sized kitchen, living room and dining room, a southern facing sunroom and a maid's room off the kitchen (They used it as a TV room). The lot included a three-car garage with apartment above and work shop in back, looking out at the mouth of the Amityville River. Grandma and Grandpa Kontur occupied

13.16 Kurt Nezbeda at the helm of the Marauder.
Photo courtesy Kurt Nezbeda.

the guest house, a small cottage back near the boat slip. We used to play baseball on the lot across the street which was the estate arboretum when the house was built. That property did not go with the sale to the Nezbedas and stayed vacant, later developed with two houses.

I spent a lot of time at the Ocean Avenue house through our grade school and high school years. Mr. Nezbeda was a quiet man of above average height with broad shoulders and a hawk nose. He treated all of us kids with respect and was considered one of the "good guy" parents in the neighborhood. The house was a haven for building projects with a good wood shop in the basement, the work shop behind the garage and plenty of set-up space in the three-car garage.

The biggest project was the California ski boat Kurt and his dad built in the garage. This bad boy, aptly named *Marauder*, featured a Chevrolet 283 cubic inch engine developing 220 horsepower. I watched the progress as they laid the keel, set the ribs, applied the plywood and finished it with fiberglass. The engine sat in the stern so Kurt and his dad had to engineer the "V" drive that ran forward in the boat then back aft to create the proper shaft angle. What a boat to water ski behind!

Another notable project was the restoration of a 1951 MG TD. They bought the iconic, vintage car and set about restoring it with all stock parts and paint except for the solid walnut

13.17 Kurt Nezbeda in his restored 1951 MG TD.

dashboard supplied by a woodworker friend. They used to hang a wreath on the spare tire in the back at Christmastime. Kurt told us all that the car was for him but his dad was not so quick to give it up. Kurt still keeps that car street registered at his home in Savannah, GA, the original red paint job changed to yellow.

Ed Nezbeda had studied the violin as a boy and developed a love of music which he carried with him all his life. The Ocean Avenue house boasted both a piano and a Hammond organ and the family (except for Kurt) shared his love; Blanche played the spinet and sang and their daughter, Karen, sang and played both the piano and organ. Nezbeda had such a drive to master the organ that he took lessons from Mildred Alexander, a world renowned organist, arranger and teacher. One of Alexander's proudest accomplishments was the year she was on staff at the Radio City Music Hall where she was the only woman to have served in that position.

When Ed had learned as much as he could from Millie Alexander he sought help from Dick Liebert the chief organist for Radio City Music Hall. Liebert would hold that position for forty years. Nezbeda was certainly serious about his passion. As I write this I feel a loss; for all the time I spent at the Nezbeda home I never heard him play.

Karen fondly remembers her Dad sitting next to her on the piano bench, and later, the organ bench, while she practiced her lessons; precious time between father and daughter. His influence was strong and Karen became an accomplished musician in adulthood. Ed had a dream of finding a small church pipe organ and installing it in the sun room at home. That promised to be difficult but he had plans to install the pipes and wind chest beneath the sun room floor. Not the first engineering challenge in his life.

After college my wife and I were living in upstate New York. We had traveled back to Amityville for the holidays in 1969 and I stopped by to visit with Kurt. He wasn't home but I had a nice chat with his dad. The conversation turned to Cindy's and my newfound passion for country auctions in search of antiques. Ed Nezbeda was a gun collector and he asked that if I ever came across a Parker shotgun to buy it for him, regardless of condition or price. He also shared with me his dream of going on a camera safari to Africa.

Not long after our Amityville visit Ed was diagnosed with cancer. Grumman kept two beds at the Mayo Clinic for use by employees faced with serious illness and Ed made the trip only to find the cancer was inoperable. He died March 24th, 1971, just two days after his 54th birthday. I never found him that shotgun and he never took that camera safari. He had found a pipe organ but was too sick to make that happen.

He was around in April of 1970 to see the drama of Apollo 13 when Grumman's LM became the lifeboat to bring the astronauts home from the near catastrophic accident on their way to the moon. It was LM #7 (the Grumman production crew called it Lucky #7) that saved the day. A proud time for Nezbeda and his crew that built the Lunar Module.

* *

Kurt Nezbeda followed his father to Grumman in 1967 after graduating from Bucknell. It was the natural move for a kid with aviation fuel in his veins. Dad had set him up with summer jobs through college so Grumman was a familiar place. Kurt tells a humorous story of his first day on the job one summer. The plant foreman told him to grab a bucket and follow him. He was led to a pigeon coop that was the plant manager's

13.18 A midnight photo of the entire F111A sub-assembly production and engineering team after the job completion on August 24th, 1964. Kurt, a summer grunt, and his dad are at the center of the group. Ed Nezbeda had just been named corporate vice president and head of manufacturing. Photo courtesy Kurt Nezbeda.

pride and joy. His assignment was to clean the pigeon coop so it would pass a promised "white glove" inspection by the plant manager himself. Kurt worked and fretted all day in the hot summer sun getting a grudging nod from the plant manager at the end of the day. Kurt arrived at the dinner table that night covered in sweat and pigeon droppings, to the horror of his mother. His dad inquired about his first day on the job knowing full well the task he was assigned. Kurt assumes his father set up the whole thing as a not so subtle way to discourage his youthful interest in working with his hands.

Kurt began his career with Grumman on summer work first in the engine department and then as a "rivet bucker" on the F111A project where Grumman produced the aft section of the F111A for General Dynamics, the lead contractor on the project.

After college Kurt started at Grumman on the Mohawk project, a plane designed for the Army's use during Vietnam. He was uncomfortable in staff positions wanting always to be up close and personal to an airplane, any airplane. Kurt found his place as a planning engineer and estimator doing work for both the F14 and E2C programs as well as light planes and Gulfstream. In January of 1978 Kurt joined the Gulfstream group and was transferred to Savannah, Georgia, Gulfstream's production location.

Gulfstream was the result of Grumman's long time dream to diversify the business away from military aircraft. The GI was a 12 passenger, low-wing, turboprop, corporate aircraft that first flew in August of 1958 and was the first in a line of industry leading corporate aircraft. The GII followed in 1966, a larger, jet-powered aircraft accommodating up to 19 passengers and capable of cross Atlantic flight. Production was moved to Savannah in 1967 to "split its...business into military and civilian division..." This was for public consumption. The driving force was actually a Long Island politician who pressed the issue that the GII, a commercial aircraft, was being built in Plant #2, the Government built facility in Bethpage.

In 1972 Grumman merged the Gulfstream business with American Aviation to become Grumman American Aviation with Grumman retaining an 80% ownership position. In a surprise move Grumman sold Gulfstream in 1978. Having lusted for a viable, commercial aircraft business to balance its heavy military volume, it is hard to understand why Grumman management would let the business go. It appears the corporate aircraft market had slowed some in 1978 due, in part, to stockholder pushback over the cost/value argument of corporate jets and the price of jet fuel resulting from the Middle East crisis. All this while Grumman was looking for cash to cover some failed new ventures. Following the sale, the corporate jet market quickly regained its upward growth and the new Gulfstream became the acknowledged leader in business aircraft, a position it continues to hold today.

Kurt Nezbeda took the new job in 1978 with Gulfstream as a Grumman majority owned subsidiary but reported to Savannah with Gulfstream on the road to private ownership. He would become the business manager for flight operations which managed

13.19.Gulfstream GI   13.20.Gulfstream GII

flight demonstrations for prospective buyers and production test flights. Kurt held
that position for 20+ years, retiring in 2003 with some interesting insight into many of
America's self-proclaimed, high-flying royalty.

Grumman's end was rather inglorious. Roy Grumman's conservative philosophy
pervaded the organization, even after his retirement, and as a company they were hard
pressed to prosper beyond their piston and propellor mentality. The F14 Tomcat program
nearly put them into bankruptcy- it was a great aircraft but they suffered with a poorly
negotiated contract with the Navy, and their success with the Lunar Lander never put
them in a position to become a primary contractor in the aerospace industry. Believing
entirely in internal growth they avoided acquisition and, in 1994, fell prey to the 'eat or
be eaten' rule of the corporate jungle and were acquired by Northrop, becoming the lesser
half of the new Northrup Grumman. Northrup quickly moved all manufacturing to more
labor friendly states; Long Island, once the leader in military aircraft manufacturing, no
longer produces a single plane.

Today, Grumman's Bethpage location is a ghost town with just 300 or so engineers
working on top secret military planning and the Grumman History Center staffed by ex
Grumman volunteers. A lone F14 Tomcat stands proudly beside the shuttered plant #2 as
a reminder of Grumman's time in the sun.

13.21 The Grumman F-14 Tomcat, in swept-wing mode, sits adjacent to the shuttered plant #2 in Bethpage.

CHAPTER 14- REPUBLIC AVIATION AND PHIL BRICE

About halfway between our house and the Nezbeda's was the Brice's, at the corner of Ocean Avenue and Bourdette Place. The large Victorian house fronted on Ocean Avenue and the wrap-around porch looked out on the street and the river beyond. Phil and his wife, Ginny, had four daughters, Phyllis, Dede, Marcia and Barbie and a lone son, Steve, fourth in the birth order. Steve and I were friends during grade school although he was

14.1 Republic Aviation in Farmingdale, L.I.

two years my junior. His dad had a great
workshop in the basement and we spent a
lot of time there with various projects.

His dad, Phil, was an aeronautical
engineer with Republic Aviation, the
other local company significantly engaged
in supplying aircraft to the military
during World War II. Republic began

14.2 Republic P-35s in formation.

as the Seversky Aircraft Company in 1931, the brainchild of Alexander de Seversky a
Russian emigre and ex-WWI pilot. Their early years were a test in airplane design and
navigating the military protocols to get an order. In 1935, in preparation for that first
order, they moved into the production facility in Farmingdale just vacated by Grumman
as they moved to Bethpage for more space. Unlike Grumman, Seversky set its sights on
land-based aircraft for the Army Air Corps. The first order came in 1936 for their P-35, an
Army fighter plane.

With their nose in the Army tent they spent quality time on aircraft development
and in 1937 offered their AP-4, a revised single-seat fighter but lost out to the Curtis P-40.
However, the Army liked what they saw and awarded Seversky a contract for 13 planes

even though Curtis got the bulk of the
business. That wasn't enough to keep
Seversky afloat and after losing $550,000
in 1939, Seversky was forced out of
the business which was reorganized as
Republic Aviation with Wallace Kellet as
president. The AP-4 was re-numbered

14.3 Republic's P47D Thunderbolt.

"DELIVERY FLIGHT" by John Hammer

FLYAWAY...Upwheeling to thunder westward in delivery flight, pursuit interceptors for the United States Army Air Forces depart from Republic Aviation's flying field at an ever increasing rate—symbolizing the tremendous expansion of the nation's aerial might. Republic Aviation Corporation, Farmingdale, L. I., N. Y., U. S. A.

REPUBLIC
AVIATION

REPUBLIC AVIATION

14.4 Republic Aviation ad from 1942

the P-43 Lancer and 272[1] were produced for the Army with 108 aircraft going to China to fight the Japanese.

In 1942 the Army took delivery of the first of the Republic designed P-47 Thunderbolts. This would be the last of Republic's propeller fighters but the largest production of fighter planes, of any manufacturer, for the war effort. The initial orders were so large Republic was forced to expand their production facilities by a factor of four and build an additional three runways. By the war's end in 1945, when the Army cancelled all open orders, Republic had produced 15,660 Thunderbolts.

The Thunderbolts provided escort service for the B-29 bombers heading to Germany. To add range for these thirsty fighters Republic engineered under-belly aluminum tanks

14.5 Our humble catamaran made with Republic P47 belly fuel tanks, ca 1958.

---

1   http://en.wikipedia.org/wiki/Republic_Aviation

to carry additional fuel for the long journey. As kids we used to play in a great old barn that sat on the back corner of the Brice property. Phil Brice had taken a bunch of those half-tanks and stacked them up next to the barn. The shells looked like kayaks to me so we took two back to my house and Steve Brice, Bruce Edwards and I fashioned a rudimentary catamaran with plywood decking, centerboard, rudder and rigging and sailed it behind our house on the Amityville River. It didn't sail very well but it was a great project. The picture is of a very young Steve Brice in the bow and an equally young Bruce Edwards in the stern, before the rigging went on.

Phil Brice had joined the company before the war just as it was transitioning to Republic. He was there to see Republic flourish in the halcyon war years. Nineteen forty-five had them reevaluating their post-war prospects with the military and looking for growth in the private sector. With the belief that the returning Army and Navy pilots would be looking to continue flying personally, they designed and developed the

14.6 The Republic F-84F Thunderjet

14.7 Republic's F-105 Thunderchief

RC-3 Seabee, a small amphibian that would sell for $3,500 to $6,000. That market never developed and they ended up selling just over 1,000 planes.

They did start development of their first jet fighter, the F-84D Thunderjet. They delivered the first 600+ mile-per-hour swept-wing version, the F-84H, in 1949 and then developed variations on the theme- the F-84F Thunderstreak was supersonic fast and another version for photo-reconnaissance was dubbed the Thunderflash.

My father-in-law, John Becak, was a Navy man during the war and spent time as a "back-seater" in a Grumman TBF torpedo bomber. After returning to Brooklyn in 1945 he applied to both Republic and Grumman. The Republic offer came in first and he started the next day. The Grumman offer followed by a day or so but he stayed on with Republic. He met Joan Wack (Grandma Joanie) at Republic, she was a telephone operator there and they were married in 1954. John was a tool and die maker for Republic and stayed there until they shut the doors in 1965, then took his tool bag to Grumman where he would eventually retire.

Phil Brice progressed to chief aeronautical engineer and at Republic's peak had 1,500 people reporting to him. In the early 1950s Alexander Kartveli, their chief designer, set out to design the Thunderjet's replacement. Steve Brice said his dad used to tell stories of lunches with Kartveli when planes were sketched out on restaurant tablecloths. The F-84 successor was the F-105A Thunderchief which became the primary ground attack aircraft in the Vietnam War. The Thunderchief held its lead dog position with the Air Force until 1970 when the McDonnell Douglas F-4 Phantom took its place.

14.8 Phil Brice
Photo courtesy Steve Brice

The 1950s were difficult years for Republic as they suffered under the feast or famine business climate managed by the military. The light-plane commercial market had not developed as anticipated and Republic was not in a position to compete for the growing airline business. In the early 1960s Sherman Fairchild began purchasing their stock and by 1965 he owned them and they became the Republic Aviation Division of Fairchild Hiller. As with Grumman, the new owners quickly moved production to their own facilities and the Farmingdale manufacturing location was shuttered. Part of the Farmingdale property is now the American Airpower Museum and they maintain artifacts from Republic including a number of the planes they produced.

REPUBLIC AVIATION AND PHIL BRICE

Phil Brice moved easily from Republic to Grumman in 1965 to work on the Lunar Lander program. He later moved to the F-14 advanced systems program until the Navy pulled the plug on that development. He retired to help his son Steve run his marine parts store in Port Jefferson, New York, a part of Steve's collection of marine related businesses which all started with his purchase of the Ocean Avenue boat yard.

CHAPTER 15- BRUCE PARKER, MR. WATER SKIING

The sport of water skiing is relatively modern which makes sense when you realize that the first motor powered launch came into use in 1885 and was only capable of six miles per hour. Motor boat speeds reached fifteen miles per hour by the end of the century, that being the necessary precursor for someone to come up with the idea of skiing on water.

That inventive soul turned out to be Captain J. L. LeRoy of the Coronado Hotel in Coronado Beach, California. Captain LeRoy was manager of the hotel's boathouse in the early 1900s and organized fishing trips and water outings for hotel guests. The story goes that following a summer cruise and day of fishing the guests relaxed with a deep sea swim. When it was time to return to the hotel one of the swimmers refused to come out of the water and told Captain LeRoy he would have to tow him to shore. The captain tossed the swimmer a wooden top to a large fish box with some line attached and began the journey back to the hotel. The towee asked for another length of rope which he tied to his make-shift life raft and used it for stability so he could stand while being towed. The sport of aquaplaning was born.[1]

Aquaplaning, or "planking," quickly became the new rage and was a popular

---

[1]   Desmond, Kevin, *The Golden Age of Water-Skiing:* (MBI Publishing Company, St. Paul, MN, 2001), 23.

Bruce Parker, Mr. Water Skiing

recreation at summer resorts around the globe. By the mid-teens it had become a competitive sport with "plank-gliding" races seen at the Scarborough Health Spa in Yorkshire, England in 1914 and "aqua planers" contests on Long Island in 1915.[2]

Could the move from one board, the aquaplane, to two boards be far behind?

Many would claim to be the first to water ski on two skis including Count Maximillian Pulaski from the Cote d'Azur Yacht Club (1929), Emil Peterson, Nice, France (1932) and Fred Waller of Huntington, Long Island, who patented a twin-aquaplane system in 1924 aptly named "Dolphin Akwa-Skees." The Pope brothers, of future Cypress Gardens fame, promoted Waller's Akwa-Skees in Florida starting in 1929.

But the honor of water ski invention goes to Ralph Samuelson of unlikely Lake City, Minnesota. In 1922 he began experimenting with snow skis behind a power boat (unsuccessfully) and finally designed a pair of wooden water skis, the first of their kind. Samuelson would also be the first to design and use a ski jump and the first to be towed by a seaplane.

By the mid-1930s the sport of water skiing had matured to the point that three distinct areas of competition had evolved- slalom, ski jump and tricks- and the sport had captured the attention of one Garden City, Long Island, boy, Harris Brewster Parker. While an undergraduate at Colgate University, Parker, Bruce to his friends, taught himself to water ski and used the process he developed to launch a school to teach the world the art of water skiing.

In 1936 Parker met Don Haines and together they developed a line of water skis and equipment. They were later joined by Charlie Tilgner, an aeronautical engineer, and the 'Bruce Parker' line of water skis was launched from Tilgner's basement. They would eventually sell the business to APCO that continued to market the popular line under the Bruce Parker name. All this while he was still in college. Right after graduation in

---

2   Ibid, 23

1938 Parker worked with Haines to put together ski troupes that performed at Jones Beach and the New York World's Fair of 1939.

During this early period Parker had a day job at Republic Aviation. Although he had elevated water skiing from a passion to a career and made the rightful claim to be the first American professional water skier, he still had to find a way to make it pay enough to support him and a family.

1939 was a defining year for Parker's career. Together with Don Haines they created the American Water Ski Association, the first national group to promote the sport. Parker assumed the position of vice president and would hold that office for ten years. Their first task was to organize the inaugural national water skiing championship held that year at Jones Beach on Long Island.

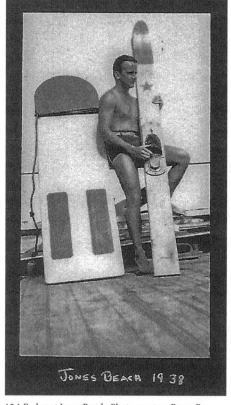

15.1 Parker at Jones Beach. Photo courtesy Bruce B. Parker

Parker won the slalom and tricks events and took the combined title. He would repeat the following year to be the back-to-back national champion. The two titles, along with his teaching activities, earned Parker the moniker "Mr. Water Skiing." All this while he was still in his early twenties.

The 1939 championships also crowned Esther Yates the women's all-around champion. Yates also worked at Republic Aviation and was a student of Parker and her

win was a feather in Parker's teaching cap.
In 1938 both Parker and Yates were hired
as stunt doubles for Madeleine Carroll
for the filming of the movie *Cafe Society*.
Carroll played a society girl from New
York and the part required scenes with her
on an aquaplane in the East River of New
York City. Yates did the double work for
the close-up shots but they used Parker,
suitably attired, to do the difficult long
shots. The student/teacher relationship
grew and evolved; Bruce and Esther were
married on New Year's Eve, 1941.

The summer before their marriage
Parker was the headline entertainment
at the Republic Aviation summer picnic.
The August 8th edition of the *Republic
Aviation News* carried this review of
Parker's exhibition:

> *The outstanding entertain-
> ment feature was the water-
> skiing exhibition of Bruce Parker,
> Republic's national water skiing
> champion. Parker made several spine-tingling transfers from a speeding boat
> to an airplane tow-line to the delight of 1500 spectators who lined the shore
> of the Great South Bay. The exhibition was covered by all leading newsreel
> companies and was distributed to theaters throughout the nation during
> the following week. Other water events included ski jumping, some of it by*

(NEWS foto)

ON THE AQUA

Bruce Parker (left) and Stanley
Powell support Esther Yates in
aquaplane ride on Fountain Lake at
the World's Fair.

15.2 Bruce and Esther performing at the New York
World's Fair, 1938

novices who made thrilling falls
and a program of speed boat races.

It is noteworthy that the event was
covered by newsreel companies and
Parker's exploits were shown to millions
of movie goers nationwide. He had
established himself as the premier water
skier in America even before making that
his singular profession.

15.3 Parker on one ski, 1938. Note the New Point Hotel
in the background. Photo courtesy Bruce B. Parker

In the early 1940s Parker set out
to create a multi-location organization
to teach America how to water ski. He
established schools at the Sagamore Hotel
in Lake George, New York, the Montauk
Yacht Club on Long Island, Dart's Lake,
in upstate New York and his home base
at the Nassau Shores Beach Club in
Amityville. For the winter months he had
schools at the McFadden Deanville Hotel
in Miami Beach and the water skiing
mecca, Cypress Gardens, in Florida. He
continued to promote water skiing for all
ages and abilities and never failed on his
guarantee to teach anyone to water ski.

By 1942 the business was growing
and Bruce and Esther left Republic and

15.6 Esther Parker. Photo courtesy Bruce B. Parker.

BRUCE PARKER, MR. WATER SKIING

15.5 Bruce Parker being pulled by a seaplane in Miami, Florida, 1946. Press photo 1/11/46.

settled in Amityville. Esther was an Amityville girl, born and raised, and they moved to a house on LeBrun Avenue, not far from her roots on Grace Court. This put Bruce close to the Great South Bay and he would manage his growing water skiing empire from Amityville. But Amityville was not ideal weather-wise for a 12 month, warm-weather enterprise and Parker was forced to follow the sun-summers in Amityville and upstate New York and winters in, first, Florida, then Nassau in the Bahamas.

The Parkers welcomed their first born, Bruce, B., in 1946 and second born, Jeff, in 1949. Both sons would become part of Dad's water skiing show, at least during summer

15.4 Chip with Dad, 1948. Photo courtesy Bruce B. Parker

vacations. Training started early. The photo shows Dad getting 2 year old young Bruce (they called him Chip) into a pair of custom made skis, taken at Parker's ski school in Nassau in 1948.

* * * * * * * * *

Parker had a nose for promotion and kept himself and his sport in the eyes of America. In 1947 he was photographed being towed by a seaplane. Not the first to pull this stunt but he laid claim to going the fastest on water skis- 70 miles per hour.

In 1949 Parker recommitted himself to the competitive circuit and over the next five years posted an impressive list of titles:

1949   U.S. National Doubles Championship with Muriel Schard

Canadian Doubles Championship with Dottie Grover

1950   World's Doubles Championship with Evie Wolford

Eastern Doubles Championship with Evie Wolford

Canadian Doubles Championship with Evie Wolford

1951   Eastern Men's Slalom Champion

U.S. National Doubles Championship with Evie Wolford

North American Doubles Championship with Evie Wolford

Canadian Doubles Championship with Evie Wolford

1952   Eastern Senior Men's Championship- Overall

Eastern Senior Men's Slalom Championship

Eastern Senior Men's Trick Championship

Eastern Doubles Championship with Evie Wolford

U.S. National Senior Men's Championship- Overall

U.S. National Doubles Championship with Evie Wolford

North American and Canadian Senior Men's Championship- Overall

North American and Canadian Senior Men's Slalom Championship

North American and Canadian Senior Men's Trick Championship

1953   Eastern Senior Men's Championship

Eastern Senior Men's Jumping Championship

Eastern Senior Men's Slalom Championship

Eastern Doubles Championship with Evie Wolford

New England Senior Men's Championship

New England Senior Men's Slalom Championship

New England Doubles Championship with Evie Wolford

Bruce Parker, Mr. Water Skiing

Beyond their impressive list of doubles championships, Parker and Evie Wolford (a Massapequa, L.I. girl) teamed up to set a distance and time record by water skiing from Nassau to Miami, twice. In June, 1952 they made the trip, 196 miles, in 8 hours and 13 minutes. In 1954 they varied the route and skied 218 miles in 9 hours and 31 minutes to establish new world records for both distance and time.

Grabbing a Bite on the Fly

Bruce Parker and Evelyn Wolford, who will attempt to water-ski non-stop from Nassau, Bahamas, to Miami, Fla., this week, try out their arrangement for taking food and drink from the towboat during the 196-mile trip across the Gulf Stream. They wear plastic shinguards to protect them from injury.

15.7 Parker and Wolford skiing from Nassau to Miami. 1952.

When we arrived in Amityville in the early '50s the Parkers lived at 53 Ocean Avenue. There is a common theme among the celebrities of Ocean Avenue and that is none was a celebrity as we would define them today; no gated mansions, no fancy cars, no egocentric lifestyles. You would be just as likely to see these folks raking leaves or running errands on the weekend than in the news. And that was a blessing for their children who were allowed the luxury of a natural childhood.

In 1955 Parker started spending summers running his ski school at Dart's Lake in New York State's Adirondack mountains. The boys spent their summers with Dad at Dart's Lake as part of the show. Young Bruce recalls that at the tender age of nine his act was doing 360 degree spins standing on a chair on a saucer (disc). He also tried the ski jump that year and ended up with a dislocated hip and full cast from waist to toe.

After three years at Dart's Lake (and a divorce from Esther) Parker moved his year-round operation to Nassau. The boys summered there and worked in the ski and snorkeling school to earn money for college. Young Bruce likes to tell the story of Lloyd Bridges and the filming of the TV series *Sea Hunt*. Parker was a stunt double for the show. He explained that when the filming started Bridges couldn't swim and had to find excuses to turn down offers to go diving with fans of the show. He finally was forced to learn to swim and it was Bruce Parker who taught him.

In the 1950s Parker teamed up with Evinrude, the outboard engine maker, to promote water skiing with a nod to the best equipment- Bruce Parker skis and Evinrude motors. The team produced a series of magazine ads and a "How To" book of water skiing appearing in 1956.

By this time Parker was a national figure with his endorsement of Hiram Walker Imperial Whiskey in magazine

Man, this is whiskey!

15.8 Bruce Parker in Imperial Whiskey ad.

ads helping insure his recognizability. He was truly a man's man with blond hair, blue eyes, a square jaw and the body of a, well, water skier.

In 1957 Parker was honored by *Sports Illustrated Magazine* when he was asked to write an article "All About Water Skiing" which acknowledged his status as "Mr. Water Skiing." The best water skiing instructor in America got to strut his stuff in the premier sports magazine in the country.

In 1965 Bruce Parker headed to the Rum Point Club on Grand Cayman in the British West Indies as owner and manager. It was said he brought "some flair and showmanship" to the club. Gone were his commuting days of summers in New York State and winters in Florida and Nassau. He added snorkeling and scuba diving to his curriculum vitae in the Bahamas but he will always be known as the guy who taught America to water ski. At last

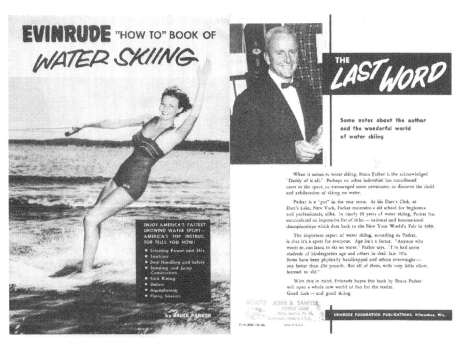

15.9 How To Book of Water Skiing, 1956, front cover   15.10 How To Book of Water Skiing, 1956, back cover

count that number was 17,000.

Along the way he boasted some celebrity students. He taught Yul Brenner to water ski and scuba dived with Hugh Downs whom he met as a guest on the Tonight Show with Jack Paar. Downs was Paar's second banana at the time. The Parkers remember a boating picnic with Steve Allen and his family following Parker's guest appearance on the Tonight Show. Steve Allen was the show's first host starting in 1954 and running to 1957 when Jack Paar took it over.

In 1983 Bruce Parker was inducted into the USA Water Ski Association Hall of Fame, the organization he helped found forty-four years before. Their tribute includes this summary of his accomplishments:

THE GOLDEN AVENUE

To millions in eastern United States during the 1930's and 40's, Bruce Parker was "Mr. Water Skiing." No individual water skier before or since has commanded the attention of the media- newspapers, magazines, newsreels, - to the extent that Parker did. Winter and Summer. Winters in Miami and the Bahamas, summers in New York. Hardly any stunt involving water skiing escaped his imaginative attention. Show skiing. Doubles acts with pretty girls. "Impossible" oceanic marathons. And, of course, competition.[3]

His sons remember him as always on the move, the master of promotion, organizing shows and events and forever the golden haired boy on water skis, reveling in his endless summer.

* *

I knew his son Bruce B. from our Ocean Avenue days in Amityville. He was born with salt water in his veins reinforced by summers working for his dad's scuba diving and water ski schools in New York and the Bahamas. He deserves an honorable mention in the list of Ocean Avenue notables for his work with NOAA and his book *The Power Of The Sea: Tsunamis, Storm Surges, Rogue Waves, and our Quest to Predict Disasters.*

From Bruce's web page:

15.11 The two Bruces, 1948. Photo courtesy Bruce B. Parker

---

3   www.usawaterskifoundation.org/#!bruce-parker/clcla, accessed 1/27/16

Bruce Parker, Mr. Water Skiing

Over the years he mixed his encounters with the sea with academic training and research, to eventually become a world-recognized expert in the oceanographic subjects covered in The Power of the Sea. He has a PhD in physical oceanography from The Johns Hopkins University, an MS in physical oceanography from the Massachusetts Institute of Technology, and a BS/BA in biology/physics from Brown University.

Before leaving NOAA (National Oceanic and Atmospheric Administration) in October 2004, Dr. Parker was Chief Scientist for the National Ocean Service, and before that Director of the Coast Survey Development Laboratory. He is presently a visiting Professor at the Center for Maritime Systems at the Stevens Institute of Technology in Hoboken, NJ. His awards include the U.S. Department of Commerce Gold Medal and Silver Medal, the NOAA Bronze Medal, and the Commodore Cooper Medal from the International Hydrographic Organization. Dr. Parker is also a former Director of the World Data Center for Oceanography, and a former principal investigator for the NOAA Global Sea Level Program, and at one time ran the U.S. tides and currents program. Dr. Parker has published over a hundred papers and articles and written or edited several books.[4]

I remember Bruce, the son, as that very bright kid who earned class valedictory honors and wore them well. Our first meeting was on a frozen Amityville River, behind our house, for a pick-up hockey game in the mid-1950s. The day ended badly with a swinging hockey stick (mine) and a chipped tooth (his). Fifty years later, while researching this book, I was relieved to find out that his boyhood nick-name "Chip" was not a reference to his tooth but to his resemblance to his father, as in "off the old block," and just possibly, an easy way to avoid the confusion of two Bruces in the same household.

---

4   Parker, Bruce B., author's web site, thepowerofthesea.com/theauthor.html, accessed 3/10/18

CHAPTER 16- THE LOMBARDOS

Late in 1962 the Lombardos moved in next door to us, the property just north on Ocean Avenue. The house was a typical mid-20th century split level, one of three in a row built in the fifties, up on Ocean Avenue, with no access to the river. Myton Ireland, of the founding Irelands, had built a house next to ours on the river, in the late 1950s, and the Lombardo house sat in front. There was Lebert, his wife Peggy, daughters Liz, about six or seven years old, Gina and son, Carmen, just a toddler.

16.1 The Lombardos from 1943. From left to right, Guy, Victor, Lebert and Carmen with 17 year-old Rose Marie in the middle.

Lebert Lombardo was the brother of Guy Lombardo and part of the family business, Guy Lombardo and The Royal Canadians. The Lombardo brothers- Guy, Carmen, Lebert and Victor- were first generation Canadians born in London, Ontario. Guy formed his first musical group when they were in their teens and by 1924 had created The Royal Canadians with his three brothers and a group of local musicians.

Beginning in 1924 the orchestra
was actively recording, starting with
Vocalion, then Columbia, Brunswick,
Decca and Victor. They adopted a smooth
style and described themselves as "The
Sweetest Music This Side of Heaven."
They gravitated to New York City where
the orchestra set up shop in the Roosevelt
Grill at the Roosevelt Hotel from 1929
to 1959. It is from New York, in 1928,
that the Royal Canadians gave their first
New Year's Eve big band remote radio
broadcast that became as much a part
of America's New Year's Eve celebration

16.2 An autographed press photograph of Lebert Lombardo.

as champagne and noise makers. The radio remotes became TV remotes in the 50s and
continued from the Roosevelt Grill until 1959, then from the Waldorf Astoria until
1976.[1,2] They were noted for playing the traditional *Auld Lang Syne* as the Times Square
ball dropped and Guy Lombardo got the moniker "Mr. New Year's Eve." Even today it is
the Royal Canadians' recording of *Auld Lang Syne* played first in New York's Times Square
at the New Year.

The Royal Canadians were popular and prolific. From the period 1927 to 1954
they released 200 singles with 111 making it to the top 10 and 24 going all the way to

---

1   Guy Lombardo died in 1977 but the program continued on for a few years succumbing finally to *Dick Clark's New Year's Rockin' Eve.*

2   Who can forget the live cut-aways from *Johnny Carson's Tonight Show* to *Ben Gauer at Times Square* to watch the ball drop.

number 1. Some notable number one singles are *Charmaine* (1927), *By the River St. Marie* (1931), *Stars Fell on Alabama* (1934), *Red Sails in the Sunset* (1935), *It Looks Like Rain in Cherry Blossom Lane* (1937), *Penny Serenade* (1939), *Managua, Nicaragua* (1947) and *The Third Man Theme* (1950).[3] Brother Carmen did most of the orchestration and much of the writing with Lebert on lead trumpet. In the 1937 hit *It Looks Like Rain in Cherry Blossom Lane*, Lebert did a rare and delightful job as the vocalist. For most of the orchestra's existence, Kenny Gardner was the lead singer with a sweet tenor voice and the perfect match for their "sweet" sound. He was "discovered" by their sister, Rose Marie, whom he married, adding Kenny to the family business.

16.3 A Lebert Lombardo solo vocal release. One that didn't make the charts.

For all this fame the Lombardos were just regular folks and friendly neighbors. Home from college in the summer of '64, my sister, Betty, dragged me next door to meet the new neighbors. Kenny Gardner and his wife Rose Marie were there and were frequent visitors to the Ocean Avenue home. "Uncle Kenny" as my sister called the crooner, was sitting on the front steps drinking a beer. Lebert had set up a ping-pong table in the single car garage and I was soon challenged to a match by Uncle Kenny. I think I beat him. This all seemed so strange because my mother still remembered swooning to Kenny Gardner's

---

3   http://www.musicvf.com/Guy+Lombardo+and+His+Royal+Canadians.art, accessed 11/10/2017

dulcet tones at the Roosevelt Grill when she and dad were young marrieds. While our new neighbors and the rest of our family had moved comfortably past the Lombardo's fame, our mother had not.

In 1952 Robert Moses completed the Jones Beach Marine Theater, the last piece of his most famous Jones Beach State Park. The Marine Theater was an amphitheater sitting on the edge of Zach's Bay with the stage separated from the audience by a moat. The actors had to be transported to the stage by boat and often times the scenery was floated around the stage. The opening musical was *A Night in Venice* by Johann Strauss II and produced by Mike Todd. It was a terrific start with Enzo Stuarti in the lead, supported by floating gondolas, no less.

Robert Moses had built the theater with Guy Lombardo in mind to run it. Moses was an ardent fan of Lombardo and his Royal Canadians and used the theater extensively for entertaining his political friends and foes. A typical day for his guests was a swim in the ocean at Moses' private section of Jones Beach then a dinner in his private dining room,

16.4 The Jones Beach Marine Theater production of Mike Todd's *A Night in Venice*, 1962

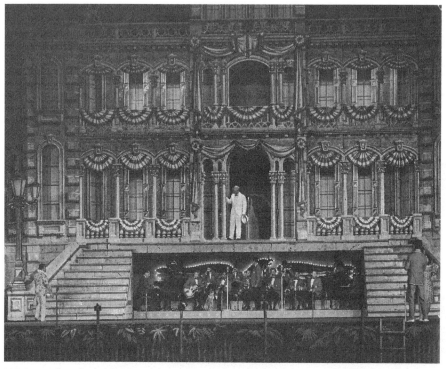

16.5 A press photo for the 1961-2 production of *Paradise Island* showing Guy Lombardo and his Royal (Hawaiians) Canadians in the orchestra pit.

attended to by his personal chef, then an evening at one of Moses' private boxes at the Marine Theater. Moses would make a personal appearance at the beginning of the show, just in time to be presented to the audience by Guy Lombardo and spend a few minutes with his guests, then adjourn to a private office to put in a few hours of work.[4]

My sister, Betty, developed a close relationship with Liz and used to regale us with stories of her trips with Liz and her dad. The show at the Marine Theater in 1965 was *Mardi Gras* with Louis Armstrong the featured performer. Lebert took Liz, 8, and Betty, 10, to one of the early performances with a promise they would get to meet the

---

4   Caro, Robert A., *The Power Broker, Robert Moses and the Fall of New York*: (Vintage Books, a division of Random House, New York, 1975), 816-17.

16.6 A photo of the Royal Canadians with Guy Lombardo's autograph. Lebert is on the first trumpet just to the left of Guy Lombardo's head.

famous Louis Armstrong. Armstrong and Guy Lombardo had developed a professional relationship over the years. Armstrong had made the public statement that the Royal Canadians was his favorite orchestra and this raised the hair on the necks of jazz performers and enthusiasts who thought the mellow sound of the Royal Canadians was better fit for elevators. Armstrong was also quoted as saying that for his band in Heaven he wanted Lebert to play lead trumpet. He said he liked the way Lebert held the melody, a not so subtle poke at the more progressive and celebrated trumpeters of their day.

The visit to the Marine Theater that day was not all that Betty had hoped. While she did get to see Guy Lombardo's office with "a bar that came out of the wall" they only got to see Louis Armstrong from across the room as a horde of reporters and photographers mobbed the star and blocked their way.

Mom and Dad had been invited to the opening of *Mardi Gras!* that year by Lebert. The night would include cocktails and dinner at Guy Lombardo's restaurant in Freeport, L.I., transportation to the Marine Theater aboard Guy Lombardo's yacht, V.I.P. treatment at the show and a nightcap back at Lombardo's restaurant. Mom and Dad declined the invitation citing a previous engagement, which happened to be a local cocktail party they could have easily missed. I was amazed they passed up such a wonderful opportunity. I would later understand their reluctance to be part of an entourage that included the who's who of New York's political and social elite, most likely including Robert Moses, Guy Lombardo's patron saint. The Long Island south bay people had no love for Robert Moses.

I was a sailing instructor at the Unqua Corinthian Yacht Club that first summer the Lombardos moved to Ocean Avenue. Lebert asked if I would give his daughter, Liz, private sailing lessons. I was delighted at the chance to earn a few extra dollars for college expenses. Lebert had explained that Liz was a shy child with a fear of the water. Lebert had bought the house on Ocean Avenue because he was able to negotiate the use of a boat slip on the Amityville River on the north side of the Ireland property. He kept a 30 foot sloop there and Liz was afraid to sail the bay with the family. So the "sailing lessons" for Liz were actually evening sails on the river in a small dingy the Lombardos owned. The winds were calm in the evening and we could enjoy (me more than Liz) a low-stress hour or so on the river. I didn't get around to teaching Liz much about the skills of sailing a small boat but I was able to get her a bit more comfortable on the water.[5]

The Lombardo story we love to tell is the time Lebert and family took off on vacation

---

5   It is interesting that Myton Ireland eventually retired to Sanibel Island, Florida, where he owned and operated a marina and restaurant. He chose his front door neighbor, Liz Lombardo, to manage the marina for him.

and asked mom to keep an eye on the house for them. There had been a power outage and mom stopped in to see if everything was all right. The basement freezer was off and all the meat had begun to thaw. Gracie ran to the front door and hailed a passing Amityville police car. Jumping into action the young policeman sprinted to the front door where mother loaded his arms with defrosting roasts and chops and told him to take them home to his wife, she would know what to do. She then called all the neighbors and divvied up the remaining bounty, keeping some choice cuts for herself. I returned home from college for the Thanksgiving break and was treated to some great roast beef sandwiches compliments of the Lombardos.

Mom finally came around to thinking of the Lombardos as solid Ocean Avenue folk.

Some time after our family moved from Amityville the Lombardos bought the Trieber house further south on Ocean Avenue. The house was between the Nezbeda's and the Palmer house which proudly stood at the foot of Ocean Avenue. It was a lovely, early 20th Century home boasting a pool and boat house. It would appear that the Lombardo's first Ocean Avenue house was just a temporary residence until the right waterfront property came along.

CHAPTER 17- BEAUTY...

In 1960 the Rileys moved to 112 Ocean Avenue. The house was a stately Dutch Colonial built in the mid 1920s. Waterfront lots were getting scarce by then and the builder had to turn the house sideways to fit it on the slender property. The front door looked south at the next door house built by John Ireland, Amityville luminary, 30 years before.

Christine Riley was eleven years old in 1960. She was 'girl next door' pretty with wide set eyes and prominent cheekbones that the TV camera would find irresistible in the years to come. She was a pleasant

17.1 Christine Belford in a 1972 press photo.

child and became friends with the pre-teen tribe of northern Ocean Avenue residents.

Following graduation from high school in 1966, Christine enrolled at Hofstra University in nearby Hempstead, Long Island, with the intention of studying psychology. There she got her first taste of acting under professor Joseph Leon the noted Broadway, TV and film actor. In 1970 Christine moved to New York City and did some modeling but no acting. Later that year she moved to LA for "personal and professional" reasons. She would later explain the move was to follow an unnamed actor but that relationship did not last.

So, when in Rome... Prompted by her actress friend Carrie Snodgress, Christine took a screen test with Universal Pictures and sufficiently impressed star maker Monique James to land a seven year contract with Universal. Her first credited appearance was in the movie *Vanished* in 1971.

It was also in 1971 that Christine, now with the stage name Belford, appeared in an episode of *Ironside* and her three decade career as a television actor was launched. In 1972 she appeared in two movies, *Pocket Money* with Paul Newman and *The Groundstar Conspiracy* with George Peppard, and six TV series including; *The Sixth Sense, Cool Million, Alias Smith and Jones, Owen Marshall, Counselor at Law, Mannix* and my favorite, *Banacek*. We can guess that Christine's work with George Peppard in *The Groundstar Conspiracy* gave her the inside track to playing Peppard's opposite in six episodes of *Banacek*. She played the insurance company's investigator trying to beat private investigator Peppard to the stolen loot and save his exorbitant fee. She never did. It was her work in *Banacek* that established Belford as a TV first- stringer.

Other movie credits include Stephen King's *Christine* in 1983 and *The Ladies Club* in 1986. But television was her best stage; in all she appeared in a dozen made for TV movies and sixty-four different television series. Her TV movies include; *Vanished* (1971), *The Million Dollar Rip-Off* (1976), *To Kill a Cop* (1978), *Colorado C.I.* (1978), *High Midnight* (1979), *Kenny Rogers the Gambler* (1980), *Desperate Voyage* (1980), *The Neighborhood* (1982), *Sparkling Cyanide* (1983), *Mr. and Mrs. Ryan* (1986), *The Woman Who Sinned* (1991) and *Ruffian* (2007).

Her highlight list of TV series include; *Owen Marshall Counselor at Law* (1971-72), *Mannix* (1972), *The Six Million Dollar Man* (1974), *Banacek* (1972-74), *Marcus Welby, M.D.* (1970-74), *Wonder Woman* (1976), *Battlestar Galactica* (1978), *Barnaby Jones*

(1973-79), *Married: The First Year* (1979), *The Incredible Hulk* (1979-81), *Insight* (1974-82), *Dynasty* (1982), *Fantasy Island* (1983-84), *Empire* (1984), *Silver Spoons* (1982-87), *Outlaws* (1986-87), *Murder, She Wrote* (1984-93) and *Beverly Hills, 90210* (1991-98).

Christine married veteran actor Nicholas Pryor in 1993 and remained active in her television work. As of this writing her last credit was for an appearance in the TV movie *Ruffian* in 2007.

CHAPTER 18- ...AND THE BEAST

In 1965 Christine Riley's parents divorced and the Dutch colonial house at 112 Ocean Avenue went on the market. On June 28th Ronald DeFeo Sr. and his wife, Louise, closed on the house and moved in with their four children- Ronald Jr., 13, Dawn, 9, Alison, 4, and Mark, 3. Louise was pregnant with their fifth child. They believed it would be a new beginning for the family. They were wrong.

The nearly 300 pound "Big Ronnie" DeFeo was service manager at the Brigante-Karl Buick dealership in Brooklyn, owned by his father-in-law Michael Brigante, Sr. The dealership had reputed ties to organized crime through Carl Gambino, legendary Mafia crime boss. Big Ronnie's brother was Pete DeFeo a capo in the Genovese crime family. Not exactly the kind of blood lines the waspy Ocean Avenue neighbors liked to boast of.

And the DeFeos lived up to the negative expectations of the conservative Amityville community. They were loud and unrefined. Big Ronnie was both verbally and physically abusive to his wife and children and publicly displayed an accelerating anger management problem. As a group they were the poster family for dysfunction. They had named the Ocean Avenue house "High Hopes" to signal a new beginning but by all appearances they had merely transported their Brooklyn culture and lifestyle to Amityville.

By 1974 Ron Jr. (Butch), then 23, was on probation for stealing an outboard motor and routinely abused alcohol and drugs, namely speed and heroin. His sister, Dawn, at 19 was using speed, LSD, mescaline and Quaaludes. Both children, it seems, needed the drugs to escape the realities of life under the father's tyranny.

In the early morning hours of November 13, 1974 the entire DeFeo family was murdered, except for Ronald DeFeo Jr. who claimed to have found them, all shot while sleeping. Two days later Ronald DeFeo Jr. confessed to the murders and pointed the police to the murder weapon, his high powered rifle which had been tossed in the Amityville River from the village dock at the foot of Ocean Avenue. He was arraigned that day, November 15th, 1974, for the murders of his mother, father and four siblings.

DeFeo was convicted of the six murders on November 21, 1975, just a year after the gruesome crime. He was sentenced to 6 concurrent terms of 25 years to life.

The house, the street and the village have never been the same but it is the back-story that has so damaged Amityville's reputation. It is not a story of murder but of greed and judicial sleaze.

It all began with Michael Brigante hiring a lawyer to represent his grandson. Jacob Siegfried was faced with a most difficult task. The prosecution had a signed confession and the murder weapon. DeFeo claimed the confession was obtained without his access to counsel and was beaten out of him. Siegfried petitioned the court to have the confession thrown out but the judge ruled in favor of the prosecution, believing in the credibility of the police over DeFeo. Following this, Siegfried advised DeFeo he should consider a defense of "mental defect," the insanity plea. DeFeo threatened Siegfried with bodily harm causing Siegfried to think better of pursuing this "fools errand" and withdrew from the case.

DeFeo was then given a court appointed attorney, William Weber, from the firm of Fredrick Mars and Bernard Burton, of Patchogue, Long Island. Although Weber was faced with the same problem of the confession and physical evidence, he seems to have had thoughts of a creative solution from the start.

In June of 2000 Ric Osuna was contacted by a woman claiming to be the wife of Ronald DeFeo Jr. at the time of the the murders. Osuna had a history with the DeFeo murders story, having co-produced the History Channel's documentary of the murders

and managing the most extensive web site on the subject, *The Amityville Murders*.
Geraldine Romandoe convinced Osuna that she and Butch DeFeo eloped in 1970
and produced a child born in 1974 just before the murders. It was through Geraldine
Romandoe DeFeo that Ric Osuna made contact with Butch DeFeo and authored *The Night
The DeFeo's Died*[1], published in 2002, an attempt, the author claims, to get at the "truth" of
the DeFeo murders.[2]

Whether or not we choose to believe Geraldine DeFeo's story, and many do not,
she was the catalyst for Osuna's research and subsequent book which presents new
information about the events following the murders and how the book *The Amityville
Horror* came to be written.

The plot appears to have been hatched at a meeting between William Weber and
George and Kathy Lutz in Amityville in the Fall of 1975. Weber had called the meeting
to enlist the Lutz's help in creating a story to support an insanity plea for the defendant.
The Lutzes were the eventual authors of *The Amityville Horror*. Per Geraldine DeFeo,
this was the first time the idea of the Lutzes moving into the house "to experience the
forces there"[3] was discussed. Faced with the prosecution's strong case Weber needed some
help convincing a jury that his client was insane. He also had the problem that his client
was reluctant to use the insanity defense. Geraldine DeFeo is quoted, "Because Butch
felt insulted that his insanity could be questioned, Weber had to convince him by other
means. He promised Butch that he'd get out in two to three years, and that he'd be rich
from the book's success."[4]

This was happening as the trial was in progress. Weber seemed to expect the trial to

---

1   Osuna, Ric, *The Night The DeFeos Died*, (Noble Kai Media, Nevada, United States), 2002

2   From the very beginning there existed some physical evidence that suggested DeFeo could not
have committed all six murders without assistance. This led to a number of alternative theories for the murders
furthered by variations of the story told by DeFeo himself.

3   Osuna, 260

4   Osuna, 259

drag on but the court wanted to get it over and done. The trial began on October 14th 1975 and DeFeo was convicted on November 21st, the same year. Weber announced he would appeal. On December 5th DeFeo was sentenced to 6 concurrent terms of 25 years to life.

Not quite two weeks later George and Kathy Lutz moved into 112 Ocean Avenue with their two children. The plan was in motion because William Weber still needed help with the appeal. On January 16th, 1976, the Lutz family moved out of the house. Let the games begin.

February 14th was kick-off day. William Weber formed a corporation to manage the book that he had asked George and Kathy Lutz to write. The corporation consisted of Weber, as president, Paul Hoffman, who would write the book, and Burton and Mars from Weber's law firm. Also on that day Paul Hoffman wrote the first article in what was to be an orchestrated publicity campaign. The article, "DeFeo Home Abandoned. Buyer calls it haunted." appeared in *Newsday*.

The next salvo was a news conference on February 16th with Weber and the Lutzes presenting their "true story" of being driven out of the Ocean Avenue house. George Lutz claimed, "No objects flew around: there was no wailing. But we moved out because of concerns for our personal safety as a family. There is a very strong force in there." William Weber added, "Facts supplied by the Lutzes and physical evidence brought to our attention put some of the evidence in our favor."[5] Sounds like Weber was already practicing his closing arguments for the appeal.

In March Weber sent a book contract to the Lutzes. It called for 40% of the proceeds to go to Hoffman, the author, and 12% each to Weber and four other lawyers from his firm[6]. That didn't leave anything for the Lutzes and there was language in the contract requiring the Lutzes to warrant that the events in the book were true. The Lutzes walked

---

5   Osuna, 262

6   Osuna, 265

on the deal and chose to work with Jay Anson instead. Anson was going to give them half.

As Anson was getting the book ready, Paul Hoffman authored a second article about the Lutzes vacating the Ocean Avenue house which appeared in *Good Housekeeping* in April, 1977 and the *New York Sunday News* in July of 1977. The Lutzes cried foul (is there no honor among thieves?) and sued Hoffman, Weber, Burton, Mars, Good Housekeeping, the New York Sunday News and the Hearst Corporation citing "invasion of privacy, misappropriation of name for trade purposes and negligent infliction of mental distress." They were obviously trying to protect "their story" which would publish as *The Amityville Horror* in September of 1977.

Not to be out lawyered, Weber, Hoffman and Burton counter-sued the Lutzes citing fraud and breach of contract.

In September of 1979 Judge Jack Weinstein, in a fit of judicial sanity, dismissed the Lutzes suit against Weber, et al. noting, "Based on what I have heard, it appears to me that to a large extent the book is a work of fiction, relying in large part upon the suggestion of Mr. Weber." He added further, "There is a very serious ethical question when lawyers become literary agents."[7] Judge Weinstein did allow the counter-suit against the Lutzes to continue which appears to have been settled out of court with some monies paid by the Lutzes to William Weber. Weber's publishing antics were submitted to the New York State Bar Association for review but no action was taken.

So, with all of that legal sleaze, there was no appeal, and Ronald DeFeo Jr. remains in jail. He did appear before the parole board in 1999, his first opportunity to do so, telling yet a different version of the events of November 13th, 1974 (including his innocence) to an unbelieving parole board. His parole was denied. He remains held at the Sullivan Correctional Facility in Fallsburg, New York.

The sad story is that this grand hoax, conceived and implemented to aid the defense

---

7   Osuna, 266

of a convicted mass murderer, produced a book, *The Amityville Horror*, that captivated American readers and spawned countless magazine and newspaper articles, numerous television documentaries and, at current count[8], eleven movies, all based on a fraud. To this day the house at 112 Ocean Avenue and the Village of Amityville continue to suffer from the indignity imposed by this hoax. The two words, Amityville and Horror, are inextricably linked. Ask anyone on the street about the Amityville Horror and they will tell you it was real. It said so in the book. They can't lie about that, can they?

---

8   The eleventh movie in the Amityville Horror series, *Amityville, The Awakening,* was released in 2017.

Chapter 19- A River Tour-
a Good Beginning, a Better Ending

I began researching this book in 2015 after publishing *My Amityville*. I needed to get serious about my research and took my first trip to Amityville in September to spend some time at the Amityville Historical Society and start the interviewing process. While

19.1 Looking south from Steve Brice's front porch. Yacht Service Inc. is in the right center of the photo and Wilbur's Island is in the background.

recounting this trip to my second son, Chis, he reminded me that he had never been to Amityville. Our family moved away in 1966 and we never took the kids back. He was the biggest supporter of my new literary calling and expressed a strong desire to get to know the Amityville where I was raised and share my rediscovery process. The trip was on.

19.2 The author with Steve Brice at the helm.

We arrived at 132 Ocean Avenue on a warm and brilliant October afternoon. We were meeting Steve Brice at his home, just north of Yacht Service, Inc. the boatyard he had owned and operated most of his adult life. I had coerced Steve into giving us a tour of Amityville by boat- the best way for Chris to get to know the Amityville of my youth. Steve's son was running the boatyard then and lived in the family home up on Ocean Avenue. Steve and his wife had built their new home at the water's edge, looking south toward the mouth of the Amityville River.

19.3 Ireland's Mill ca. 1910, looking north from the head of the Amityville River. The Ireland homestead is out of the picture on the left.

Chris and I stood on Steve's front steps and looked south across the stern of his classic sloop *Busman's Holiday* at

19.4 Mariner Park looking south. Faust's Campus Nook sat here in the '50s and '60s and the ocean ferries loaded at this dock at the turn of the century.

the boatyard with its forest of masts, all
aluminum now, and the sea of fiberglass
boats ready for winter storage. Wilbur's
Island sat pointing toward the mouth of
the river and the Great South Bay beyond.
I was home.

We boarded Steve's 1978, 22-foot
Chris Craft and headed north on the
river. Steve piloted us to the head
of the river; we would start the tour

19.7 This 1920s postcard looking south at Wilbur's Island
is nearly identical to the photo I took from Steve Brice's
porch one hundred years later.

appropriately at the beginning, both of the river and the history of Ocean Avenue. The
boat came to rest in the still water looking to the north. I struggled with three conflicting
images in my head- what I was seeing now, strong memories of my youth and softer
images of what my mind created of the early days, aided by old photos and vintage
postcards.

What I was looking at, straight ahead, was a complex of apartment buildings on the
north side of Merrick Road, the creek now relegated to a subterranean path to the river.
My mind's eye saw the early 1900s Ireland mill sitting on the east side of the mill pond
and the Ireland homestead sitting back from the road on the west side of the creek. What
I remembered was the Ireland home still there in the '50s with the new Memorial High
School just to the east. Memories of wading in the creek and catching huge, golden carp in
our bare hands flashed in my mind.

At the turn of the century the west side of the river was the boarding place for ferries
to the ocean beaches. For a few years, up to 1910, the Cross Island Trolley stopped here
at Ocean Avenue and Merrick Road for passengers connecting to the ferries. In my
time the Fausts operated the Campus Nook on this spot, a luncheonette favored by high
school students. Today the property is the village Nautical Park established in 2003 and

maintained by the village as a tribute to
its nautical history.

We turned and started south, slowly,
enjoying the day. Straight ahead was
Enoch Island, the first island in the river
to be created by the 1892 dredging.
Prominent on the north end of the island
is the house built by Rufie and Nita
Ireland, new since my high school days.

19.5 Enoch Island looking south from the head of the
Amityville River

Accessible only by boat, the building permit was delayed by questions from the Amityville
Fire Department over who would respond and how a house fire would be handled. A part
of the Ireland family mill was used in the construction, somehow saved all those years
since the mill was closed in 1929.

We moved around the west side of the island, preferring the more scenic Ocean
Avenue side of the river to the dredged, western channel. Facing westward on Enoch
Island, just south of the Ireland house, is the rustic home built by Lou Howard. Lou is
an Amityville legend. I knew him as my driver's ed teacher and varsity football coach.
His teams won nine consecutive league championships and Lou still holds the New
York State high school record for the highest win/loss percentage. He earned a Ph.D in

19.6 The Lou Howard built home on Enoch Island

aerospace technology and helped SUNY
Farmingdale develop their aerospace
program and served as its first chairman.
He dabbled in politics as well, serving as
Amityville's trustee then mayor, Presiding
Officer of the Suffolk County Legislature
and New York State Assemblyman. He
also took a turn as publisher and owner

A River Tour- a Good Beginning, a Better Ending

of *The Amityville Record* and *The Suffolk County News*. Lou was named to the Town of Babylon's ten most influential people of the 20th Century. We called him Uncle Lou.

Continuing south we cleared Enoch Island and spotted the Riley/DeFeo house on the eastern shore, looking none too forbidding in the bright afternoon sun. The many owners since the Lutz's book shared only one complaint- the lack of privacy from ghost hunters and supernatural thrill seekers. The next house south was the Ireland home, built by John Ireland in the early days of the 20th Century. Rufie and Nita Ireland lived there before building on Enoch Island.

We continued south coming up on the central part of the river and Ocean Avenue where the boat builders plied their trade. Looking across the river to the west bank I saw Owen Brooks's boathouse and home, about even with Island #2 and Wilber Ketcham's workshop.

We were back to where our day started. My mind played tricks again, flashing between what I was seeing, what I remembered and what I could imagine the area looked like a hundred years ago. Wilbur's Island looked remarkably the same with dilapidated boathouses surrounded by hundreds of boats already out of the water for the winter. Wilbur's boathouse and shop were still there, an unofficial monument to his time. The island itself is slowly eroding with the relentless action of the tides, its eventual demise insured by the very bureaucrats entrusted to protect it.

Heinley's coal yard, the Wicks property and the Ocean Avenue Boatyard had been merged over the years to become Yacht Service, Inc. but the look was much the same with shiny fiberglass boats replacing the painted and varnished wooden craft of the first half of the 20th Century. As we passed the southern tip of Wilbur's Island we came up on the house that Annie Oakley rented and I could almost see her out in back, practicing her shooting over the river.

We had passed the mid-point of the river and were approaching home territory for me. It was hard to picture this area as all marshes and cat tails and salt hay before the residential development started. This most familiar territory for me started where Gil Haight lived and kept the *Commodore*, the iconic Wicks built Great South Bay schooner.

Just to the south, still on the western shore, was the Kennedy home, a relatively new ranch style home from the 1950s. Bruce Kennedy was two years behind me in school and stayed in Amityville becoming the village attorney. He and his wife still live in the family home on the river. Next door was the Wheeler house, then the house Myton and Dolly Ireland built in the late '50s. The Lombardos lived up on Ocean Avenue, behind the Ireland home.

Our house at 260 Ocean Avenue was built in the mid-twenties by Treadwell Ketcham, a New York financier, who lived there until we bought the house in 1953. It literally sat on the water; the sun porch built over an old boat slip. The VanHoff boathouse sat adjacent to the north and housed their boat *Moxie*, a wooden cabin cruiser of the old and elegant style. After fifty years the house and boathouse looked just the same.

19.8 260 Ocean Ave. looking good in 2015 despite a bad time with hurricane Sandy.

A RIVER TOUR- A GOOD BEGINNING, A BETTER ENDING

Directly across the river is the Ronback house. Jack was one of the last of the baymen, making his living dredging, building docks and any construction projects requiring access from the water. His son, Randy, lives there now and continues the family business.

Missing, though, was Our Island. For over a hundred years it sat there, directly across from our house, the first thing we saw out the back door. Dad used to hit golf balls over there and I paddled our Blue Jay over on race days to put her on her side and scrub the bottom clean. The small but substantial island- fifteen yards wide and forty yards long- had been washed away by years of hurricane action, Sandy being the final straw. All that was left was a tree branch stuck in the river bottom to mark the now shallow spot.

Still heading south we passed the site of the Gilbert Rod and Gun Club on the east bank of the river, just across from the Hearns homestead and where John Hearns kept the

19.9 A pre-WWI photo of the Hearns clan aboard the *Pudge* with the Gilbert Rod and Gun Club in the background. The children include John and his sister, Rosemary, peeking out the window. Photo courtesy of Charles (Bucky) Parker.

19.10 The Hathaway Inn and New Point Hotel ca. 1910.

19.11 The Palmer House at the foot of Ocean Avenue, in 2015, as viewed from Ocean Avenue.

A River Tour- a Good Beginning, a Better Ending

Pilgrim. The family home sat up on Ocean Avenue and was sold in the early '60s, but John kept the waterfront property and summered on a houseboat there for a few years. The Rod and Gun Club was built in 1884 for the use of a group of wealthy Brooklynites when the east side of the river was largely uninhabited. It was long gone when we arrived in town.

As we approached the mouth of the river the O'Malley house was on the right with the Nezbeda house next door looking old and tired. I looked left, half expecting to see the grand old New Point Hotel. It had dominated the eastern shore until it burned in 1962. Just eleven years later its sister hotel, the Hathaway Inn, suffered the same fate.

Back on the western shore, just south of the Nezbeda's, was the Trieber house, where the Lombardos moved in the 1970s, then the Palmer House, still the most iconic Victorian structure on Ocean Avenue. It was on this spot the Ocean Point Hotel was built in the 1880s, adjacent to the village dock.

As we continued south past the village dock I could picture the Narragansett Hotel, a little ragged and unappreciated in my youth, now a bunch of contemporary homes stood there. But this was a wonderful place in the teens and twenties with an active village dock, a thriving hotel, O'Brien's beach and the Sperry boathouse and testing grounds just to the

19.12 The Narragansett Inn looking southwest from the Amityville River ca. 1910. The village dock is to the right. The UCYC clubhouse is in the far left background.

19.13 The Unqua Corinthian Yacht Club in the early 1900s. Photo courtesy the Unqua Corinthian Yacht Club.

south. I could almost see Sperry making his test flights over the bay..

We continued south into the Great South Bay and turned west around the dock of the Unqua Corinthian Yacht Club. The land was a gift from John Ireland in 1900. The club had been such an integral part of the village's history it seemed a fitting end to the river tour. The docks had been expanded since my time, the porches enclosed and a swimming pool added. It was a far cry from its humble beginnings; a simple clubhouse and dock sitting on the eastern most edge of the original West Neck.

* *

In all, we travelled about a mile by water, just an hour or so. What started out as a fun afternoon, a backyard view of the street I grew up on, had taken on greater significance. The book that I envisioned, this book, began as a collection of stories and memories of some interesting folks associated with Ocean Avenue. There was still much research to do and I still had much to learn about the street I knew as a boy, but this hour long cruise began to establish an outline and a timeline for the narrative to follow.

The themes began to clarify: early commerce established with the Ireland Mill and Heinley's coal yard, the boat builders, pioneers in aviation, the hospitality industry, ferries to the ocean beaches, the impact of Prohibition, aviation manufacturing in the war years, those that entertained us. What was first an unnamed muddy access path to the creek and salt hay meadows became an avenue of fine homes. Teamed with the river it shadowed, they witnessed the one hundred year transition from commerce to hospitality to upscale residential living. A century of family histories- sixty homes, or so, and a wealth of stories about interesting people- people who became the fabric and legends of Amityville.

But they were more than that. They were pioneers who influenced the history of our nation.

Sadly, these rich histories are known to very few these days. The mill is gone and with it all but one of the Ocean Avenue commercial properties that fueled the early village growth. The craft of wooden boat building is now just a romantic notion, replaced by technology and mechanization. The creative energies of early aviation were dimmed with the untimely death of Lawrence Sperry, his epic achievements now dwarfed by the awesome state of modern aviation. And the vibrant adolescent years of aviation, so much a part of Long Island's great industrial history and the winning of World War II, were lost to a welcome peace and the vicissitudes of corporate America. Grumman and Republic are remembered today only as places where a relative once worked. The grand hotels all met fiery ends and were not replaced and, along with the ocean ferries, were casualties of the automobile and the new lifestyle it allowed and promoted. The coming of the automobile was also the reason the Cross-Island Trolley failed and a root cause for O'Malley's dilemma with his Dodgers. Radio as an entertainment source has almost disappeared, overpowered first by television and now the magic of portable music. The rest of the Ocean Avenue luminaries moved on in one way or another. But their stories should be forever part of the celebration of Ocean Avenue and Amityville, and the greater history of America as well.

BIBLIOGRAPHY

AMITYVILLE AND LONG ISLAND HISTORY

Amityville Historical Society, *Images of America: Amityville*, Arcadia Publishing, Charleston, South Carolina. 2006.

Bailey, Paul (editor), *Long Island; A History of Two Great Counties, Nassau and Suffolk*, Volume 1, 1949.

Brewster-Walker, Sandi, "Frances Hunter Fowler, caterer for Al *Capone*," *The Amityville Record*, Amityville, NY. 1/21/2015.

Caro, Robert A., *The Power Broker, Robert Moses and the Fall of New York*: Vintage Books, a division of Random House, New York, 1975.

Christin, Pierre and Balez, Oliver, *Robert Moses, The Master Builder of New York City*: Nobrow (US) Inc., 2014.

Klein, Karen Mormando, *Postcard History Series: Amityville*: Arcadia Publishing, Charleston, South Carolina, 2012.

Lauder, William T., *Amityville History Revisited*: The Amityville Historical Society, 1992.

Lauder, William T., *Eulogy for the Commodore*, Historical Supplement to the Amityville Historical Society Dispatch.

Martin, Humbert O. Jr., "The Seaford Skiff," *The Amityville Record*, Amityville, NY, date unknown.

Niemi, Victoria, *Boat Building in Amityville*: The Department of History, Stony Brook University, Fall 2002/Spring 2003.

Perrin, Janet and Howlett, Charles F., *A Walk Through History; A Community Named Amityville*: Heart of the Lakes Publishing, Interlake, New York, 1993.

Robinson, Doug, *My Amityville, Memories of a Golden Time*: self published, 2015.

Seyfried, Vincent F., *The Cross-Island Line: The Story of the Huntington Railroad*: Garden City, L. I., 1976.

Sweeney, Kate, *The Streets of Amityville: Wood Avenue is Not Named for the Forest*, Amityville Historical Society, 2006.

Thomas, Barry, "The Melon Seed and the Seaford Skiff:" *The Log of Mystic Seaport*, Summer, 1974.

Thompson, Benjamin F, *The History Of Long Island From Its Discovery And Settlement To The Present Time, Volume 1*: first published in 1843, reprint 2015, Facsimile Publisher 103 DDA Market Ashok Vihar, Phase 3, Delhi, India.

Tooker, William Wallace, *The Indian Names For Long Island With Historical And Ethnological Notes*: First published in 1909, reprint 2015 in India by Facsimile Publisher, Delhi.

VanNostrand, Roy, *Wilbur Ketcham Testimonial Dinner*, October 8, 1965, Pamphlet reprinted 8/13/1983 as a memento of the 50th Anniversary of the founding of the Narrasketuck Yacht Club.

PROHIBITION AND THE RUM WARS

Allen, Everett S., *The Black Ships, Rumrunners of Prohibition*: Commonwealth Editions, 1979.

Behr, Edward, *Prohibition, Thirteen Years That Changed America*: Arcade Publishing, 1996.

Brewster-Walker, Sandi, "Frances Hunter Fowler, caterer for Al Capone," *The Amityville Record*, Amityville, NY. 1/21/2015.

Canny, Donald L., Coast Guard Bicentennial Series, "Rum War: The U.S. Coast Guard and Prohibition," United States Coast Guard web site.

Kobler, John, Capone, *The Life and World of Al Capone*: Da Capo Press, 1971.

Kobler, John, *Ardent Spirits, The Rise and Fall of Prohibition*: Da Capo Press, 1993.

Lauder, William T., *Lawrence B. Sperry, Sr., A Man of Parts*: Amityville Historical Society, The Dispatch, No. 3, 2016.

Waters, Harold, *Smugglers of Spirits, Prohibition and the Coast Guard Patrol*: Hastings House, Publishers, New York, 1971.

Willoughby, Malcolm, F., *Rum War at Sea*: Treasury Department, United States Coast Guard, Washington, 1964.

EARLY FLIGHT ON LONG ISLAND

Bilstein, Rodger E., *Flight in America 1900-1983*: The Johns Hopkins University Press, Baltimore and London, 1984.

Clear, Ellen, Honoring Grumman and its Hellcat, *The New York Times*, 1/5/1986, http://www.nytimes.com/1986/01/05/nyregion/honoring-grumman-and-its-hellcat.html?mcubz=3

Davenport, William Wyatt, *Gyro! The Life and Times of Lawrence Sperry*: Charles Scribner's Sons, New York, 1978.

Gulfstream Aerospace, Wikipedia, http://en.wikipedia.org/wiki/Gulfstream_Aerospace.

Gulfstream History, Pioneering Business Aviation, Company History.

Grumman Aircraft Engineering Corporation, Annual Report for 1949.

Gunston, Bill, *Grumman: Sixty Years of Excellence*: Orion Books, New York, 1988.

"Lawrence B. Sperry Makes Night Flight Demonstration." *Aerial Age Weekly*, September (9/11/1916), p. 777.

Kelly, Thomas J., *Moon Lander: How We Developed the Apollo Lunar Module*: Smithsonian Books, Washington and New York, 2001.

Lauder, William T., *Lawrence B. Sperry, Sr., A Man of Parts: Amityville Historical Society*

Loening, Grover, *Takeoff Into Greatness, How American Aviation Grew So Big So Fast*: G.P. Putnam's Sons, New York, 1968.

Republic Aviation, http://en.wikipedia.org/wiki/Republic_Aviation.

The Dispatch, No. 3, 2016. Loening, Grover, *Takeoff Into Greatness, How American Aviation Grew So Big So Fast*: G.P. Putnam's Sons, New York, 1968.

"This Day in Aviation, 2 September 1944," Grumman Aircraft Engineering Corporation Archives, http://www.thisdayinaviation.com/tag/grumman-aircraft-engineering-corporation/

Scheck, William, "Lawrence Sperry: Genius on Autopilot." *Aviation History*, November

2004

Skurla, George M. and Gregory, William H.: *Inside the Iron Works: How Grumman's Glory Days Faded*: Naval Institute Press, Annapolis, Maryland, 2004.

Stoff, Joshua, *Long Island Aircraft Manufacturers*: Arcadia Publishing, Charleston, South Carolina, 2010.

Thruelsen, Richard, *The Grumman Story*: Praeger Publishers, New York, 1976.

WALTER O'MALLEY AND THE DODGERS

D"Antonio, Michael, *Forever Blue, The True Story of Walter O'Malley, Baseball's Most Controversial Owner, And the Dodgers of Brooklyn and Los Angeles*: Riverbed books, New York, 2009.

Goldstein, Richard, *Superstars and Screwballs: 100 Years of Brooklyn Baseball*: Dutton, 1991.

"The Dodger's Walter O'Malley," *Time*, Vol. LXXI No. 17, April 28, 1958.

THE DEFEO MURDERS

Anson, Jay, *The Amityville Horror, A True Story*: Bantam Books, New York, 1977.

Osuna, Ric, *The Night The DeFeos Died*: Noble Kai Media, Nevada, 2003.

ANNIE OAKLEY

Buffalo Bill Museum, http:collections.centerofthewest.org/treasures/view/disc_brass_oakley_annie_each_disc_stamped_one_side_shot_withaumc_car2

Fields, Armond, *Fred Stone: Circus Performer and Musical Comedy Star*: McFarland & Company, Inc, 2002.

Fred Stone, https//en.wikipedia.org/wiki/Fred_Stone.

Kasper, Shirl, *Annie Oakley*: University of Oklahoma Press, 1992.

"United States." *Time Magazine*, December 6, 1926. "From Greenville , Ohio, I received a heavy brown pasteboard box, which I carried to the stage of the Globe Theatre, Manhattan, and opened in the presence of a notary public. It contained several scrapbooks, with clippings, photographs, letters and a typed autobiography up to 1890 of my late friend, Annie Oakley Butler, ablest markswoman in history, who died last month. There was no letter of explanation but it seemed apparent that Annie Oakley, with whom I played in a circus some 20 years ago, wished me to be her Boswell."

Stone, Fred, *Rolling Stone*: Whittlesey House, A division of McGraw-Hill Book Company, Inc., New York and London 1945.

THE GAMBLINGS OF WOR RADIO
Gambling, John B., https://en.wikipedia.org/wiki/John_B._Gambling

Gambling, John A., https://en.wikipedia.org/wiki/John_A._Gambling.

Gambling, John R., https://en.wikipedia.org/wiki/John_R._Gambling.

Hinckley, David, *From fill-in to star: How Morning exercise host John B. Gambling became NYC's first radio personality*, New York Daily News, 8/14/2017.

Kahn, Toby, "John B. Gambling begat John A. Gambling who begat John R. Gambling and that's How Radio's Oldest Dynasty Was Born", *People Magazine*, 1/28/1985

Ketcham, Diane, "About Long Island; At Home on Morning Radio", *New York Times*, 1/20/1991.

Radio Guide, An Illustrated Weekly of Programs and Personalities, Vol. 1, No. 6, New York, 12/5/1931.

OTHER SOURCES FOR OCEAN AVENUE RESIDENTS
Desmond, Kevin, *The Golden Age of Water-Skiing*: MBI Publishing Company, St. Paul, MN, 2001.

Gladstone, Henry; Radio Newscaster, 83, *New York Times*, 1/27/1995,

www.nytimes.com/1995/01/27/obituaries/hrnry-gladstone-radio-newscaster-83.html.

Guy Lombardo and His Royal Canadians, www.musicvf.com/Guy+Lombardo+and+His+Royal+Canadians.art.

Off Came the White Gloves: Much to Christine Belford's relief, *TV Guide*, April 28, 1973

Parker, Bruce, "All About WATER SKIING" *Sports Illustrated*. August 19, 1957.

WOR (AM), https://en.wikipedia.org/wiki/WOR_(AM)

Parker, Bruce, B., author's web site, thepowerofthesea.com/theauthor.html

USA Water Ski Foundation, www.waterskifoundation.org/#!bruce-parker/clcla, accessed 1/27/16

.

Made in the USA
Coppell, TX
21 June 2021